# TOP **10**
# SCOTLAND

# CONTENTS

## 4

## Introducing Scotland

## 18

## Top 10 Highlights

# SCOTLAND

# INTRODUCING

*Edinburgh skyline*

# WELCOME TO
# **SCOTLAND**

**Ruggedly beautiful, rich in culture and steeped in a romantic past – it's no wonder Scotland has fuelled the passions of artists, writers and adventurers for centuries. Don't want to miss a thing? With Top 10 Scotland, you'll enjoy the very best the country has to offer.**

An epic landscape of windswept glens and hulking mountains, dotted with ruined castles and inky lochs, Scotland's Highlands are one of the last great wilderness areas of Europe. Supreme among these is the Great Glen, a huge geological fault cleaved through by four lochs – most famously deep, forbidding Loch Ness, famed for its resident monster. Far to the west lie the spectacular peaks of Skye and to the south, the bleak and beautiful valleys of Glencoe and the Cairngorms' wild uplands, all breathtaking backdrops for thrilling hiking, biking or wildlife-

**The Isle of Iona in the Inner Hebrides**

watching adventures. Equally inspirational are Scotland's cities. Stunningly sited around a series of volcanic crags, Edinburgh steals the show with its imposing castle and the Royal Mile – an ancient thoroughfare that's packed with visitors during the world-famous summer festival. A beacon of the Enlightenment, the city has the lion's share of artistic treasures, including the National Museum of Scotland and the Scottish National Gallery, yet Glasgow – home to the Kelvingrove and Riverside Museum – is its cultural match, with an upbeat energy and dynamism that outguns even the capital.

And all that just scratches the surface. From the lush Border country, home to the evocative ruins of historic abbeys and great baronial mansions, to the far-flung archipelagos of Orkney and Shetland, scattered with reminders of a fascinating Norse heritage, there are so many things that make this vibrant country irresistible.

So, where to start? With Top 10 Scotland, of course. This pocket-sized guide gets to the heart of the country with simple lists of 10, expert local knowledge and comprehensive maps, helping you turn an ordinary trip into an extraordinary one.

# THE STORY OF
# SCOTLAND

**Scotland has evolved through centuries of interaction – often violent, sometimes peaceful – with powerful neighbours to the south and across northern and western seas. Through its fluctuating fortunes, this rugged land has always maintained a proud independence of spirit. Here's the story of how it came to be.**

## Scotland Begins

Stone Age settlers arrived in Scotland around 7000 BCE. By around 2500 BCE, Neolithic folk were building impressive megalithic structures, such as the stone circles at Calanais on Lewis and the Ring of Brodgar in Orkney. By the first millennium BCE their descendants, later mythologized as the Picts, had learned to forge iron.

In 82–84 CE the Roman general Agricola led his legions deep into the land the Romans called Caledonia. He claimed victory at the Battle of Mons Graupius but his army was soon forced back to the safety of Hadrian's Wall. They made further raids in the 2nd and 3rd centuries, building the Antonine Wall between the firths of Forth and Clyde, but again failed to hold steady.

## Picts, Scots and Vikings

After the Romans abandoned Britain in 410 CE, Scotland was contested between several kingdoms; the most powerful were the Picts of the far north. Scots interlopers crossed the Irish Sea in the early 6th century, establishing their kingdom of Dal Riada in Argyll. Irish missionaries Christianized this pagan realm from their base at Iona, and after centuries of conflict Scots and Pictish lands merged to create the Kingdom of Alba in 843.

By this time Norse raiders (called "Lochlannach" by the Scots) had arrived, initially to plunder and then to settle in Orkney, Shetland and the Hebrides, where they created a uniquely creative fusion of Celtic and Norse cultures that lasted into the next millennium.

**Viking raiders on board *drakkars* (longships)**

**Mary, Queen of Scots, a Catholic in a country changing to Protestantism**

## New Invaders

In 1072, William of Normandy followed up his conquest of England by invading Scotland, ushering in centuries of cross-border warfare. In the late 13th century, Edward I of England earned his soubriquet "The Hammer of the Scots" in campaigns aimed at conquering Scotland once and for all, but he and his successor Edward II were halted by fierce resistance led first by the charismatic William Wallace, then by Robert the Bruce. Bruce's victory at Bannockburn secured Scotland's independence, but sporadic warfare between the two nations continued.

Bruce's line ended in 1371, when Robert the Steward became king, founding the Stuart dynasty. Most of his Stuart successors were ill-fated: James I and James III were assassinated, James II was blown up by his own cannon, James IV died in battle and James V perished after another defeat by the English.

## The Reformation

The Reformation arrived in Scotland during the reign of James V's daughter, Mary, Queen of Scots, creating a long rift between Catholics and Protestants. Mary was imprisoned and executed by her royal cousin, Elizabeth I, but her son, James VI, struck lucky when he succeeded to the childless Elizabeth's throne in 1603, uniting the Scottish and English crowns and reigning as James VI of Scotland and James I of England.

## Moments in History

**563 CE**

St. Columba founds a monastery on the island of Iona and spreads Christianity, easing the merging of tribes.

**843**

Scots and Pictish realms unite to create the Kingdom of Alba.

**1320**

The Declaration of Arbroath is sent to the Pope, affirming Scotland's independence following the decisive Scots victory at Bannockburn in 1314.

**1513**

The English army under the Earl of Surrey defeats an invading Scots army at Flodden; 10,000 Scots, including King James IV, are killed in battle.

**1603**

In the Union of the Crowns, James VI of Scotland succeeds to the English throne as James I.

**1707**
The Act of Union creates the United Kingdom of Great Britain; the Scottish Parliament is dissolved.

**1745-46**
Charles Edward Stuart ("Bonnie Prince Charlie") leads the final Jacobite rebellion, ending in his defeat at Culloden.

**1848**
The first steam trains run between Scotland and London.

**1914–18**
World War I claims the lives of 74,000 Scottish soldiers.

**1999**
The Scottish Parliament is reestablished after 292 years.

**2014**
Scotland votes against independence from the United Kingdom in a referendum.

## Civil War and the Act of Union

James's reign brought peace for a while, but open war between Scottish Presbyterians and his successor Charles I soon merged with England's Civil Wars. Scots fought for both sides, but Scotland ultimately picked the losing Royalist faction, becoming part of Cromwell's Commonwealth until the restoration of the monarchy. The following years were turbulent, with hard-line Protestants resisting the Catholic-leaning Charles II and his successor James II. James was ousted in 1688 by his daughter Mary II and her husband, William of Orange. His supporters, mainly Catholic Highlanders (the first "Jacobites"), rebelled, but were quickly quelled.

Scotland had till now kept its own Parliament in Edinburgh but economic collapse brought on by an unwise attempt to start its own colony in Panama forced it to agree to full union with England in 1707.

## The Birth of Modern Scotland

Support for the exiled Stuarts was finally extinguished after the failure of the second Jacobite Rebellion in 1745, and was followed by the brutal pacification of the Highlands. The end of civil strife however helped foster a new mercantile economy. The Act of

**The Battle of Culloden, which ended the 1745 Jacobite rising**

**A North Sea oil rig in the Cromarty Firth, northeast Scotland**

Union had opened up access to English markets and joining the transatlantic trade in tobacco, sugar, cotton and enslaved people brought vast wealth. In time, merchants invested in the revolutionary new technology of steam power, transforming Glasgow into a great manufacturing city. Edinburgh meanwhile became a crucible of the Enlightenment, earning the city the title of "Athens of the North".

## Scotland in the 20th Century

The Industrial Revolution had turned Scotland into an overwhelmingly urban society, with thousands moving to the cities to work in shipyards and mills. Industrial areas suffered, though, as the British economy declined after World War II.

Discovery of North Sea oil in the mid-1970s helped the economy and turned Aberdeen into a world energy capital. Oil wealth also gave Scotland increased confidence in its ability to stand alone. In 1997, a large majority of Scots voted for the reestablishment of a Scottish Parliament.

## Scotland Today

Scotland in the 21st century is a cosmopolitan and proudly inclusive society. Many Scots are descendants of 19th-century immigrants from Ireland and Italy, and many more originate from Commonwealth countries. Its same-sex marriage legislation, meanwhile, is among the most liberal in the world.

The pro-independence Scottish National Party (SNP) has governed in Scotland since 2007, and though Scots narrowly rejected independence in the referendum of 2014, Brexit – which was opposed by most Scots – ignited demands for a second attempt. Scandals and allegations of incompetence dented the SNP's appeal in the early 2020s, and the party suffered huge losses in the UK's 2024 general election. Even so, many Scots still yearn for independence, though – like a return to the EU – this seems at present a distant dream.

**Pride celebrations on Edinburgh's Royal Mile**

# TOP 10
# EXPERIENCES

**Planning the perfect trip to Scotland? Whether you're visiting for the first time or making a return trip, there are some things you simply shouldn't miss out on. To make the most of your time – and to enjoy the very best this beautiful country has to offer – be sure to add these experiences to your list.**

**1 Visit Edinburgh Castle**
Discover why Scotland's most impressive stronghold (p22) is also its most popular paid attraction. Browse its collections to take in 900 years of history and soak up panoramic views from the mighty ramparts. Be sure to be there for the firing of the One O'Clock Gun (daily except Sunday).

**2 Explore the great outdoors**
From brooding mountains to glassy lochs, Scotland is famed for its wild landscapes. Explore them by getting active: hike the West Highland Way (p56); cycle coast-to-coast on the John Muir Way (p57); or canoe Loch Ness (p36) – taking care not to disturb Nessie, of course.

**3 Nurse a dram**
The "water of life" is the essence of Scotland, and the country is still the world's biggest producer of whisky. Most pubs have a fine selection, but connoisseurs should follow Speyside's Malt Whisky Trail (p43) for tutored tastings in some of Scotland's most historic distilleries.

**4 Admire art in Glasgow**
A hub of culture, Glasgow boasts some incredible art museums. Seek out the Glasgow Boys at Kelvingrove (p30), glimpse contemporary pieces at the Gallery of Modern Art (p101) and don't miss House for an Art Lover (p102), designed by local architect Charles Rennie Mackintosh

## 5 Road trip the NC500
Arcing around Scotland's remote northern coast, this epic road trip (p38) takes in white-sand beaches, magnificent castles and tiny coastal villages. Highlights include Kylesku Bridge, an engineering marvel, and the amazing sea stacks at Duncansby Head.

## 6 Glimpse local wildlife
Spotting Scottish wildlife, elusive but ever-present, is always a thrill, whether it's dolphins in Moray Firth (p116), reintroduced beavers in Argyll or whales off the Isle of Mull. Inland, the brooding Cairngorms (p42) are home to wildcats, ptarmigan and osprey.

## 7 Take in a folk session
Countless pubs across Scotland host informal traditional music sessions. Top trad venues include Sandy Bell's in Edinburgh, Hootenanny in Inverness and the Mishnish in Tobermory (p131). The Ceilidh Place in Ullapool (p123) is also a lively spot for a traditional ceilidh.

## 8 Go wild on Skye
Spend a week on dramatic Skye (p34) and you'll remember it forever. Here you'll find the brooding, jagged mountains of the Cuillins, cute coastal settlements like Portree, and otherworldly rock formations, including the famed Old Man of Storr.

## 9 Step into history
Seek out the locations where history was made. Ponder ancient civilizations at Neolithic sites in Orkney (p134) and visit battlefields like Bannockburn (p107) and Culloden (p119) where Scottish identity was shaped, blood on steel.

## 10 Taste Scotland
Scotland may be most famous for its haggis but there's a wealth of other delicious dishes to try (p72), from creamy cullen skin to tummy-filling stovies. There are plenty of places to try it, too, from Michelin-starred restaurants to down-to-earth pubs.

# ITINERARIES

**Strolling the Royal Mile, cruising Loch Lomond or sampling whisky: there's a lot to see and do in Scotland. With places to eat, drink or simply take in the view, these itineraries offer ways to spend 2 days in Edinburgh and 7 days circuiting the country.**

## 2 DAYS IN SCOTLAND

### Day 1

#### Morning
Begin your day at Edinburgh Castle *(p22)*. A national icon, this impregnable fortress commands views in all directions over the city and out to the coast, making it the ideal orientation point. After taking in its various attractions, wander down the Royal Mile *(p24)*, the stretch of ancient streets that made up medieval Edinburgh's main thoroughfare. Those with a taste for a dram shouldn't miss a tour of the informative Scotch Whisky Experience *(p84)*, with a sharpener for a homemade soup-and-sandwich lunch at nearby Deacon's House Cafe *(304 Lawnmarket)*.

#### Afternoon
Continue along the Royal Mile, exploring key sights such as St Giles Cathedral *(p24)* where the Scottish

 **SHOP**
For handmade sweet treats, pop into the Fudge House on Canongate *(fudgehouse.co.uk)*. Try the tablet – firmer, crumblier and even more sugary than fudge, it's a delicious local alternative.

Reformation was initiated by John Knox; the firebrand preacher's house is a little further along *(p25)*. At the foot of the road, goggle at the modern architecture of the Scottish Parliament *(p24)* before taking a tour of the royal treasures and portraits on show at the Palace of Holyroodhouse *(p25)*. Returning along the street, take a walk back in time to the city's gruesome past at Real Mary King's Close *(p84)* – it's open well into the evening – before dining on innovative Scottish cuisine at The Witchery by the Castle *(p87)*.

### Day 2

#### Morning
Spend the morning admiring glorious artworks at the National *(p26)*, particularly in the new Scottish galleries where you'll see historic takes on Edinburgh sights; don't miss the excellent museum shop. From here it's a short walk across bustling Princes Street to George Street, the dignified

**The Royal Mile, overlooked by the Tron Kirk bell tower**

**The Dugald Stewart Monument, Calton Hill**

thoroughfare designed as the centrepiece of Edinburgh's Georgian New Town. Just beyond elegantly landscaped St Andrew Square, the Café Royal Circle Bar *(p86)* is an unpretentious lunch stop for a plate of oysters and other seafood treats.

## Afternoon

From George Street, head north down Dundee Street for the 20-minute walk to the restful Royal Botanic Garden *(p82)*, a vast oasis of lawns, ponds, rhododendron walks and rock gardens. After you've had your fill of impressive horticulture, jump on bus #8 from the gardens' east gate to Leith Street, a short hop from Calton Hill *(p82)*. Crowned by an eclectic assortment

of Neoclassical monuments, this much-loved vantage point is the perfect place to soak up sunset views of the Old Town, castle and Firth of Forth beyond. Cap the day with an evening along the Shore in Leith *(p57)*, a 20-minute tram ride away. Edinburgh's rejuvenated old port area is now home to the city's densest concentration of smart restaurants and easygoing bistros.

---

### ✪ EAT
Michelin-starred but unfussy, Heron *(p87)* on the Shore in Leith gives fine Scottish produce a creative makeover, with a menu slanted towards seafood.

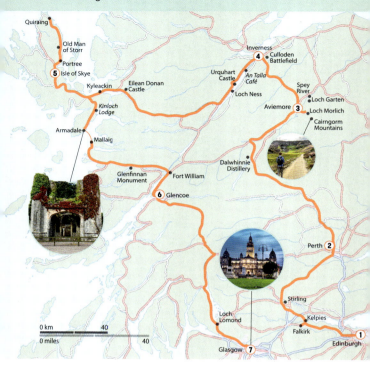

Map labels:
Quiraing
Old Man of Storr
Portree
5 Isle of Skye
Kyleackin
Eilean Donan Castle
Kinloch Lodge
Armadale
Mallaig
Glenfinnan Monument
Fort William
6 Glencoe
Inverness
4 Culloden Battlefield
Urquhart Castle
An Talla Café
Loch Ness
Spey River
Loch Garten
Aviemore 3 Loch Morlich
Cairngorm Mountains
Dalwhinnie Distillery
Perth 2
Stirling
Kelpies
Falkirk
Loch Lomond
Glasgow 7
Edinburgh 1

0 km 40
0 miles 40

# 7 DAYS IN SCOTLAND

## Day 1

Give context to the week ahead by learning all about Scottish history and culture at Edinburgh's National Museum of Scotland (p28). In the afternoon, drive northwest to Stirling, pausing en route to view the magnificent Kelpies sculptures near Falkirk. Explore Stirling's cute town centre and hilltop castle (p107) and then try Hermann's (p111) for dinner.

> **VIEW**
> Look out for Bannochburn battlefield (p107) from Stirling Castle; a battle was once fought within view of this stronghold.

## Day 2

Leave Stirling for Perth (p97). Perth Museum is home to the Stone of Scone, a national emblem once used for the coronation of monarchs. Continuing north, rolling wooded terrain gradually gives way to brooding mountains on the glorious drive into the Cairngorms. Whisky lovers shouldn't miss a late-afternoon tour at Dalwhinnie Distillery (distillerytours.scot) en route to Aviemore, the day's final stop.

## Day 3

Begin with a gentle circular forest walk around beach-fringed Loch Morlich (p42) for great views of the Cairngorms. Then drive on to the Loch Garten Nature

**EAT**
For dinner on day 4, try fresh seafood at the Red Shye Restaurant (*redshyerestaurant.co.uk*), a 10-minute drive away from Kyleachin.

Centre *(p43)* to spy these birds at their breeding site. Continue on to Inverness *(p119)* for dinner at The Mustard Seed *(p123)* and live music at Hootananny (*hootananyinverness.co.uk*).

## Day 4

Start the day with a riverside stroll in Inverness before a side-trip to poignant Culloden Battlefield *(p119)*. From here, it's just a 20-minute drive to Dochgarroch Lock, starting point for boat trips on Loch Ness *(p36)*. After lunch, hop back behind the wheel for the two-hour drive on to Skye. The road hugs a series of dramatic lochs, with two iconic castles en route: Urquhart *(p36)* and Eilean Donan *(p121)*. Spend the night at Kyleakin.

## Day 5

Get up early and spend the whole day exploring Skye. In the morning, visit the wonderful rock formations of the

**Eilean Donan Castle, the Western Highlands**

Old Man of Storr and the Quiraing *(p34)*, then spend a lazy afternoon ambling around Portree. In the early evening, take the ferry across to Mallaig and drive down to Fort William, via the Glenfinnan monument and viaduct *(p120)*.

## Day 6

Set off early to see Glencoe *(p121)* in the full splendour of the morning light on your drive to Glasgow. Break the journey at the pretty village of Luss on Loch Lomond, where you can hop on a lake cruise. Once settled in to Scotland's biggest city, choose from any of our recommendations *(p105)* for dinner – perhaps Mother India for a break from Scottish cuisine.

## Day 7

Spend the morning exploring Glasgow Cathedral and its magnificent Necropolis *(p101)*, then wander west to bustling, pedestrianized Sauchiehall Street. Have lunch at Mackintosh at the Willow *(p104)*, in Charles Rennie Mackintosh's original Tea Rooms building. Get better acquainted with the designer's work at the Kelvingrove *(p30)*, Glasgow's finest museum, and then finish with dinner at Ubiquitous Chip *(p105)* and live music at the brilliant Clutha *(Stockwell St)*.

# TOP 10 HIGHLIGHTS

*The Old Man of Storr, Isle of Skye*

# EXPLORE THE
# HIGHLIGHTS

There are some sights in Scotland
you simply shouldn't miss, and it's
these attractions that make the
Top 10. Discover what makes each
one a must-see on the following pages.

Port of Ness

Seisiadar

*Isle of
Lewis*

Tarbert

Gairloch

Uig

❻

Elgol

Mallaig

*Inner Hebrides*

Coll

Tiree

*Isle of
Mull*

*Atlantic
Ocean*

Jura

Islay

Campbeltown

❶ Edinburgh Castle

❷ Scottish National
Gallery

❸ National Museum
of Scotland

❹ Kelvingrove Art Gallery
and Museum

❺ Riverside Museum

❻ Isle of Skye

❼ Loch Ness and the
Great Glen

❽ North Coast 500

❾ Culzean Castle

❿ The Cairngorms

*North
Channel*

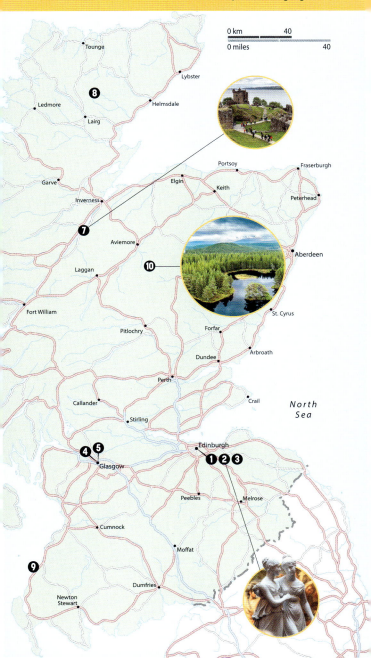

0 km 40
0 miles 40

Tounge

Lybster

❽

Ledmore

Helmsdale

Lairg

Portsoy

Fraserburgh

Garve

Elgin

Keith

Peterhead

Inverness

❼

Aviemore

Aberdeen

❿

Laggan

Fort William

St. Cyrus

Pitlochry

Forfar

Dundee

Arbroath

Perth

Callander

Crail

Stirling

*North
Sea*

Edinburgh

❹❺

❶❷❸

Glasgow

Peebles

Melrose

Cumnock

Moffat

❾

Dumfries

Newton
Stewart

# EDINBURGH CASTLE

⬛ M4 ⬛ Castle Hill ⬛ Apr–Sep: 9:30am–6pm daily; Oct–Mar: 9:30am–5pm daily (last adm: 1 hr before closing) ⬛ 25 Dec & Boxing Day ⬛ edinburgh castle.scot ⬛⬛

**Dominating the city's skyline since the 12th century, this hilltop stronghold has played various roles throughout its history, including royal palace, barracks, prison and parliament. Today, this national icon is one of the country's most popular visitor attractions and home to the glittering Scottish crown jewels.**

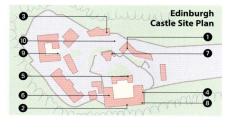

**Edinburgh Castle Site Plan**

offers spectacular views. Don't miss the One O'Clock Gun, fired here every day except Sunday from a great 25-pounder cannon.

## 1 Gatehouse and Portcullis Gate

The gatehouse was built in 1886–8, more for its looks than functionality. The two bronze statues are of William Wallace and Robert the Bruce *(p9)*. The original entrance was via the formidable Portcullis Gate of around 1574.

## 2 Argyle Battery

The northern defence of the castle

## 3 Great Hall

Constructed around 1500, this hall features Scotland's oldest wooden roof and probably its most magnificent. The open-timber roof is supported on projecting stone corbels, with intricate little carvings. The Great Hall was the meeting place of the Scottish Parliament until 1639.

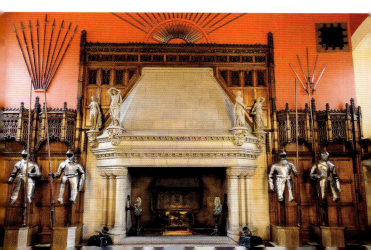

**The majestic Edinburgh Castle**

### 4 Crown Jewels

The UK's oldest crown jewels have lain here since about 1615. Made up of the royal Crown, Sceptre and Sword of state, they have been worn by Stewart monarchs including James V and I and his daughter Mary, Queen of Scots.

### 5 Scottish National War Memorial

The National War Memorial lists all of Scotland's war dead since 1914. Exterior carvings include a phoenix, symbol of the surviving spirit.

### 6 Prison Vaults

During the 18th and 19th centuries, the castle's vaults were used to hold French prisoners of war.

> **EAT**
> Pop into the lovely Tea Rooms, located in the heart of the castle's Crown Square, for fresh scones and coffee. The afternoon tea is truly excellent.

**Exhibits on display in the Great Hall**

---

> **TOP TIP**
>
> Go on a witty guided tour or take an informative multilingual audio tour.

Their graffiti can still be seen, as can the objects they made, such as bone dyes for forging banknotes.

### 7 St Margaret's Chapel

This tiny, charmingly simple building is the oldest structure surviving from the medieval castle. Probably built by David I in honour of his sanctified mother, it is still used today, and contains some wonderful stained glass.

### 8 Royal Palace

Here in 1566, in a small panelled chamber, Mary Queen of Scots gave birth to James VI, the first king to rule both Scotland and England.

### 9 Governor's House

This elegant house is beautifully

---

proportioned. It can only be viewed from the outside, as it is still reserved for ceremonial use.

### 10 Mons Meg

A cannon of awesome proportions, Mons Meg sits outside St Margaret's Chapel. Built in Belgium in 1449, it could fire a 150-kg (330-lb) stone ball over 3.5 km (2 miles) – cutting-edge technology in the Middle Ages.

**The Belgium-made Mons Meg cannon**

# The Royal Mile

### 1. Scottish Parliament

⚲ R3 ⬛ Canongate ⏲ 10am–4:45pm Mon, Fri & Sat, 9am–6pm Tue–Thu ⬛ parliament.scot ⬛

Designed by the late Spanish architect Enric Mirrales, the Parliament building was opened in 2004 by Queen Elizabeth II. It is well worth taking one of the tours of this architectural landmark (advance booking required).

### 2. Writers' Museum

⚲ N3 ⬛ Lady Stair's Close ⏲ 10am–5pm daily ⬛ edinburghmuseums.org.uk

Occupying Lady Stair's House, built in 1622, and set in a charming courtyard, this is the place to learn about three great Scottish writers, Robert Burns, Sir Walter Scott and Robert Louis Stevenson, through portraits, manuscripts and personal possessions.

### 3. St Giles' Cathedral

⚲ N4 ⬛ High St ⏲ 10am–6pm Mon–Fri, 9am–5pm Sat, 1–5pm Sun ⬛ stgilescathedral.org.uk

This building has been a landmark and a marvel since 1160. Near the entrance, look for the bagpiping angel, the exhilarating rib-vaulted ceiling of the Thistle Chapel and the heraldic flags. There is a self-service café and a shop here.

### 4. Historic and Ghostly Tours

Until the 18th century most residents of Edinburgh lived along and beneath the Royal Mile. The old abandoned cellars and basements, which lacked any proper water supply or ventilation,

**Signage for the popular Cadies and Witchery Tours**

were once centres of domestic life and industry. Mary King's Close is one of the most famous of these areas – its inhabitants were all killed by the plague in around 1645. In 2003 many of these closes were opened up for the first time and visits are now possible through the Real Mary King's Close (p84). Alternatively, choose an adrenalin-pumping ghost tour with City of Edinburgh Tours (cityofedinburghtours.com) or Cadies and Witchery Tours (witcherytours.com), where costumed guides lead visitors on a walking tour of the Old Town's gruesome past and haunted alleys.

### 5. Scottish Storytelling Centre

⚲ P3 ⬛ 43–5 High St ⏲ 10am–6pm daily (last adm: 5pm) ⬛ scottishstorytellingcentre.com

This is a venue for local and visiting storytellers and other exponents of the spoken word, performing traditional tales and new work in English, Scots and Gaelic. Along with live storytelling sessions, the centre also hosts theatre, music, dance, cultural events, festivals and workshops.

**Historic house of John Knox on the Royal Mile**

**THE ROYAL MILE**

The city's most historic street formed the main thoroughfare of medieval Edinburgh, linking the Edinburgh Castle to Holyroodhouse. Thronged with street performers during the festival (*p77*), it is a hub of entertainment year-round. Don't miss the narrow closes off the main street.

## 6. Museum of Childhood

Founded in 1955, this was the world's first museum of childhood (*p66*). The wonderful display includes books, games, costumes, rocking horses and dolls; the oldest item here is a Queen Anne doll from around 1740. An overhaul in 2018 saw the introduction of an interactive play space.

## 7. John Knox's House

**P3** **43–5 High St** **10am–6pm daily (last adm: 5pm)** **scottish storytellingcentre.com**

A beautiful medieval building, this was home to the great patriarch of the Scottish Reformation John Knox. One of Edinburgh's oldest surviving buildings, it is well worth exploring for its many surviving decorative details. Displays tell the story of Knox's life in the context of the political and religious upheavals of his time.

## 8. Museum of Edinburgh

**Q3** **142 Canongate** **10am–5pm daily (last adm: 4:30pm)** **edinburghmuseums.org.uk**

Set in Huntly House, this museum has a specialist local collection. A maze of rooms comprises primitive axe heads, Roman coins and all manner of historical finds gathered since the Neolithic Age.

## 9. The Palace of Holyroodhouse

**R3** **Royal Mile** **Apr–Oct: 9:30am–6pm daily; Nov–Mar: 9:30am–4:30pm daily** **rct.uk**

Known today as King Charles III's official Scottish residence, the Palace of Holyroodhouse was built by James IV in the grounds of an abbey in 1498. The state rooms are used by the king. Climb nearby Arthur's Seat in Holyrood Park for views.

## 10. Camera Obscura

**M4** **Castlehill** **Hours vary, check website** **camera-obscura.co.uk**

This historic observatory has a mirror that projects a 360-degree panorama of Edinburgh. A feat of Victorian artisanship, it still astonishes visitors who can explore over 100 exhibits. Afterwards, head to the rooftop terrace to enjoy and take snaps of the spectacular views of the city.

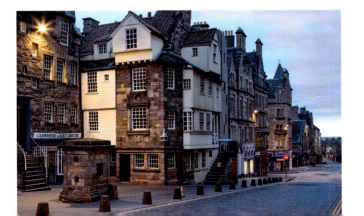

# SCOTTISH NATIONAL GALLERY

📍 M3 🏛 The Mound 🕐 10am–5pm daily 🌐 nationalgalleries.org

**Home to a world-class trove of fine art, this flagship gallery in the heart of the capital inspires and entrances with an international collection that spans over 500 years. Expect works by some of the greatest names in Western art, including Raphael and Rembrandt, as well as a uniquely rich concentration of works by Scottish masters, from Ramsay and Raeburn to Wilkie and McTaggart.**

### THE BRIDGEWATER LOAN

The Bridgewater Loan is the most important private collection of Old Master paintings loaned to public museums around the world. It includes major works by Raphael, Titian, Rembrandt and Poussin. The late sixth Duke of Sutherland offered these paintings on a long-term loan to the National Galleries of Scotland at the end of World War II. It forms the core of the gallery's display of European art.

### 1 Seven Sacraments

Depicting the rites of Christianity, the seven works evoke grand theatricality. They are considered the finest pieces by Nicolas Poussin, founder of French Classical painting.

### 2 An Old Woman Cooking Eggs

Velázquez's creation of mood through strong contrast was unprecedented in Spain when he produced this startling work in 1618. He painted this piece when he was just 18 years old.

**Velázquez's *An Old Woman Cooking Eggs***

**Artworks at the Scottish National Gallery**

### 3 The Virgin Adoring the Sleeping Christ Child

This painting's brilliant range of tones has now been revealed following careful restoration. It's an unusual Botticelli work for having been painted on canvas, not wood.

### 4 Rev Robert Walker Skating on Duddingston Loch

One of the most admired paintings by a Scottish painter, the fun-loving minister depicted by Henry Raeburn is known to have been a member of the prestigious Edinburgh Skating Club.

### 5 Dutch Collection

The pick of the best from the Dutch collection must include Rembrandt's world-weary *Self-Portrait Aged 51*, though *A Woman in Bed* also has an impressive depth of character. Dutch paintings in the galleries include works by Frans Hals, such as his lively, naturalistic *Portrait of Verdonck*.

### 6 Italian Renaissance Paintings

Works by Leonardo da Vinci and Raphael stand out here. Leonardo's *Madonna of the Yarnwinder* depicts the Christ child holding a spindle shaped like a cross, while Titian's *The Three Ages of Man* reminds us of everlasting love.

### 7 The Impressionists

You can find works by Impressionists such as Monet and Cézanne here, as well as Gauguin's *Vision of the Sermon* (Jacob Wrestling with the Angel) and Van Gogh's *Orchard in Blossom*.

### 8 Scottish Painters

The collection includes superb portraits by Ramsay, Raeburn and Guthrie, *Pitlessie Fair* by Sir David Wilkie aged 16, and *Saint Bride* by John Duncan.

Portrait of *Lady Agnew of Lochnaw*

### 9 Lady Agnew of Lochnaw

The lady's languid pose and direct gaze in this portrait caused a stir in 1892, launching her as a society beauty and giving John Singer Sargent cult status among Edwardian-era portrait painters.

### 10 Landseer's Stag

Sir Edwin Landseer's *Monarch of the Glen*, depicting a magnificent stag in a Highland setting, is known to be one of the most famous of all Victorian British paintings.

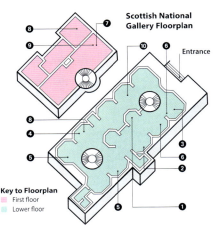

**Scottish National Gallery Floorplan**

Entrance

**Key to Floorplan**
First floor
Lower floor

🍴 **EAT**
The Scottish Café and Restaurant, located by the garden entrance, offers traditional Scottish specialities, such as Cullen shink, a rich haddock soup.

# NATIONAL MUSEUM OF SCOTLAND

🎦 N4  🏛 Chambers St  🕐 10am–5pm daily  🌐 nms.ac.uk  📷

**Offering a comprehensive look at Scottish history, this museum displays Scotland's best and rarest artifacts. The collection is housed within two radically different, adjoining buildings: here, the grand 19th-century gallery is complemented by a contemporary new wing that is one of Edinburgh's most striking modern buildings.**

National Museum of Scotland Floorplan

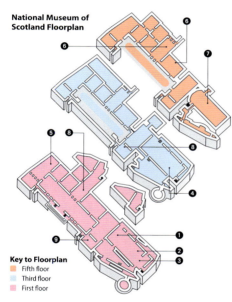

**Key to Floorplan**
- 🟧 Fifth floor
- 🟦 Third floor
- 🟥 First floor

## 3 The Maiden

This is a grisly relic to put a shiver down your spine. The Maiden was a Scottish beheading machine, which predated the French guillotine, with a weighted blade that descended from a height. It was used to behead more than 150 of those condemned in Edinburgh between 1564 and 1710, including its inventor.

## 4 Ancient Egypt Rediscovered

Covering more than 4,000 years of Egyptian history, this gallery showcases iconic objects from this ancient culture. Exhibits include a complete royal burial group as well as exquisite gold jewellery.

## 1 Lewis Chess Pieces

These enchanting ivory figures were brought to Scotland from Scandinavia by Norse merchants in the 12th century.

## 2 Monymusk Reliquary

Reliquaries were containers used for storing holy relics. The Monymusk Reliquary is connected to St Columba and Robert the Bruce, a key figure of Bannockburn *(p9)*. It dates back to the 8th century and, although it's tiny, the artisanship is exceptional. It is one of the most prized possessions of the musuem.

**Exhibit, Ancient Egypt Rediscovered gallery**

**Atrium of the Grand Gallery**

## 5 Natural History
Dinosaur skeletons and stuffed animals cascade down from the ceiling, producing spectacular visual results that almost bring them to life.

## 6 Art, Design and Fashion
This splendid gallery showcases innovation in applied arts, fashion and design. Among the many exhibits, the most eye-catching are six Wedgwood plates by Sir Eduardo Paolozzi from the 1970s and a tartan suit by Vivienne Westwood (1993).

## 7 Bonnie Prince Charlie's Canteen
Find the fugitive prince's (p120) cutlery, corkscrew, bottles, cup and condiments set here.

## 8 Science and Technology
This gallery looks at some of the country's genetic research along with its Nobel Prize-winning work on pharmaceuticals. One particularly futuristic exhibit looks at the production of state-of-the-art body implants and prosthetic limbs, developed by local company Touch Bionics.

## 9 Dolly the Sheep
A scientific marvel, the late Dolly the sheep was the first mammal cloned from an adult cell in 1996. Dolly was named after the legendary country singer Dolly Parton.

**Model of Dolly, the first cloned mammal**

## 10 The Buildings
The National Museum first opened as the Royal Museum in 1866 and has been a city landmark ever since. The atrium of the Grand Gallery, with a beautifully designed space, is worth exploring. The sandstone wing has been heralded as one of the most important constructions in postwar Scotland.

 **MUSEUM GUIDE**

Centred on the vast foyer, the older part of the National Museum is spread over three floors. Wandering the many halls can be confusing, so pick up a floor plan or ask the staff for help. The layout of the sandstone wing, accessed by the Tower Entrance, is more straightforward. The roof terrace of the Scottish Galleries offers spectacular views of the city.

**4**

# KELVINGROVE ART GALLERY AND MUSEUM

📍 Y2  🏛 Argyle St, Glasgow  🕐 10am–5pm Mon–Thu & Sat, 11am–5pm Fri & Sun  🌐 glasgowlife.org.uk/museums

**Housed in a grand Spanish Baroque building, this compelling gallery contains some 8,000 works of international significance. The collection takes in worldwide ancient cultures, as well as European and Scottish art across the centuries, and provides insights into the development of Glasgow from medieval times through to the modern day.**

### 🏛 MUSEUM GUIDE

The main collections and galleries are set out on the ground and first floors. Highlights on the ground floor are the excellent Scottish Art and Design galleries, while on the first floor the Dutch and Italian collections are particularly fine. On the lower ground floor there is a temporary gallery space reserved for major touring exhibitions, the restaurant and the main gift shop.

### 1 Miss Cranston's Tearoom

Between 1900 and 1921 the venerable Charles Rennie Mackintosh (1868–1928) was the sole designer for Catherine Cranston's tearoom empire. These beautiful interiors are of both artistic and social significance.

### 2 Spitfire

The Spitfire LA198, 602 City of Glasgow Squadron, hangs dramatically from the ceiling of the West Court. It is recognized as the best-restored warplane of its kind in the UK.

### 3 Sir Roger

Kelvingrove's most popular inhabitant is Sir Roger, a stuffed Asian elephant. Sir Roger spent the late 19th century in a travelling circus before being moved to a Glasgow zoo in 1897. It was here that the elephant lived out his final days.

**Rembrandt's *A Man in Armour***

**TOP TIP**

Daily organ recitals take place at 1pm (3pm on Sundays) in the Centre Hall.

forgotten world. It dates back to Scotland's Bronze Age (c 2500–800 BCE) and would have been used by early people living in crannogs, or loch dwellings.

## 4 Old Willie the Village Worthy

A leading figure in the group of young, rebellious Scottish artists known as the Glasgow Boys, James Guthrie (1859–1930) produced internationally significant work in the late 19th century. The *Old Willie the Village Worthy* is one of Guthrie's finest realist portraits.

## 5 Paddle Canoe

This fascinating paddle canoe, which was carved from a single piece of wood, is one of the few remaining artifacts from a

## 6 The Avant Armour

This artwork and tool of war is one of the oldest near-complete suits of armour in the world and is still in almost perfect condition. Made in Milan, a centre of armour-making, in around 1440, it is a key piece in Kelvingrove's collection.

## 7 Floating Heads

This literally head-turning art installation by Scottish artist Sophie Cave features over 50 suspended, sculpted heads, each bearing a different expression ranging from laughter to despair. Placed in the main foyer, the installation is the first thing you will encounter upon entering the Art Gallery and Museum.

## 8 Ancient Egypt

Wonders abound in the Ancient Egypt gallery, including mummies and tombs. The coffin and mummy of Egyptian lady Ankhesnefer date back to 610 BCE. Her mummified body has remained in the coffin since her funeral and burial approximately 2,500 years ago.

## 9 A Man in Armour

This fine painting by Rembrandt – a highlight of the museum's renowned collection of 17th-century Dutch and Flemish masters – is a bold depiction of a young man, probably Alexander the Great, weighed down by his armour.

## 10 Christ of St John of the Cross

Salvador Dalí's painting was first displayed in 1952. The unusual angle of the crucifixion attracted admiration, criticism and controversy, which was typical of Dalí.

**Kelvingrove Art Gallery and Museum Floorplan**

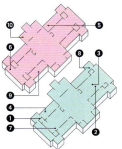

**Key to Floorplan**
First floor
Ground floor

**Spitfire on display in the West Court**

# RIVERSIDE MUSEUM

📍 Y2 🏠 100 Pointhouse Place, Glasgow 🕐 10am–5pm Mon–Thu & Sat, 11am–5pm Fri & Sun 🌐 glasgowlife.org.uk/museums 📷

**Housed in a dramatic zinc-panelled building on the side of the Clyde, this landmark museum has an extraordinary collection of trains, trams, bikes and cars. Formerly the Museum of Transport and Travel, it also considers and takes a look at the social impact transport has had on the city of Glasgow.**

**1 The Building**
Designed by the acclaimed late architect Zaha Hadid, the museum sits on the site of a former shipyard. The jagged roof of the Riverside Museum is one of the UK's most complex structures.

**2 Glasgow Tram**
Glasgow's trams achieved iconic status and were an important part of the city's culture until 1962. Step inside this original streetcar to discover stories associated with the trams and city life.

**3 South African Locomotive**
Built in Glasgow in 1945, this enormous locomotive spent more than 40 years crossing South Africa. It is the largest object in the collection and one of many restored trains.

**4 All Things Bike**
Bicycles and motorbikes on display include Graham Obree's one-hour world-record-breaking bike and the world's oldest pedal bike. A model velodrome is suspended from the ceiling.

**Glasgow's first electric tram at the museum**

The *Glenlee* beside the Riverside Museum

**VIEW**
For incredible views of the Clyde, grab a spot in the museum's café. In warmer weather you can dine outside on the terrace.

## 5 Recreated Streets

The recreated street scenes offer a fascinating insight into the city's social fabric of the time. Visitors can stroll along a cobbled and atmospheric 19th-century street, with shops, a pub, a subway station and an interactive photographer's studio.

### THE CLYDE

"Glasgow made the Clyde and the Clyde made Glasgow." After trade in sugar and tobacco expanded in the 18th century, engineers deepened the Clyde, which allowed boats to dock in the city itself, rather than unload their cargoes downriver. Shipbuilding became a major industry and Glasgow grew into the "second city" of the British Empire.

## 6 The Tall Ship

Berthed alongside the museum, the *Glenlee* is one of the five Clyde-built sailing ships that remain afloat. Built in the 19th century, it circumnavigated the globe four times. Tour the ship, and even see the captain's cabin.

## 7 The Italian Caffè

Glasgow's Italian community has been well established in the city since the 19th century. They have founded a number of much-loved cafés in the city and along the Ayrshire coast. This re-creation of a typical 1930s Italian café has chequered floors and wooden booths.

## 8 The Subway

Step into a model section of the Glasgow subway and climb aboard a carriage from an old underground train, where you can watch a short film starring 50 actors and volunteers dressed in costumes from the 1940s.

## 9 Clyde-Built Ships

The museum has over 160 models of Clyde-built ships, including luxury liners and warships. Models on display include the *Cutty Sark*, the *Lusitania* and the *Queen Mary*. There is also a World War I warship decorated with distinctive "dazzle" camouflage.

## 10 Wall of Cars

There aren't many places where you can see the first Hillman Imp, an Argyll motor and a pristine Strathclyde Police Ford Granada. A wide variety of old and new cars are on display, many of which are reminders of Glasgow's famous motor industry.

Vintage car, Wall of Cars

# ISLE OF SKYE

⚲ D2  🌐 isleofskye.com

**The largest of the Inner Hebrides, Skye is blessed with truly dramatic scenery, from volcanic plateaus to ice-sculpted peaks, croft-dotted hills to tranquil sea lochs. Beyond this, there's a collection of compelling museums, imposing castles and charming towns to explore, including pretty Portree, the island's main hub.**

**1 Loch Coruisk**
The boat from Elgol passes seal colonies to reach this lovely fresh-water loch, surrounded by the peaks of the Black Cuillins.

**2 Coral Beach, Claigan**
The pure white sand and turquoise waters of this picture-perfect beach make it appear deceptively tropical, especially on sunny summer days.

**3 Quiraing and the Old Man of Storr**
The Old Man of Storr (*p63*), a monolith created

from the erosion of a basalt plateau, is the highest and the most iconic of a series of rock formations known as the Storr. North of the Storr, the Quiraing is a landscape of towering pinnacles and high cliffs.

**4 The Cuillins**
This awesome range rises 1,000 m (3,300 ft) above the sea level. The Black Cuillins are a challenge even to seasoned climbers, but the Red Cuillins are an easier prospect for walkers.

**5 Portree**
Portree is Skye's mini capital, with some excellent shops and a delightful harbour lined with colourful buildings.

**Colourful houses lining Portree**

With stunning views of the surrounding mountains, it is an excellent base from which to explore this beautiful and rugged island.

# 6 Armadale Castle Gardens and Museum of the Isles
🌐 armdalecastle.com
Beautiful coastal gardens surround the ruined castle of Clan MacDonald, which has a historical archive.

# 7 Island of Raasay
Lying off Skye's western coast, this island is rich in flora and fauna. Visitors come for the solitude and to hike its

> ☕ **DRINK**
> The Sligachan Hotel *(sligachan. co.uk)*, near Portree, has an incredible selection of whiskies, with over 400 malts on offer from across the country.

**Dramatic rock formations of the Old Man of Storr**

rugged hills, the best of which is the 443-m (1,456-ft) Dun Caan.

# 8 Dunvegan Castle
⏱ Apr–mid-Oct: 10am–5:30pm daily 🌐 dunvegancastle.com ↗
Dramatically sited atop a rocky outcrop on the east side of Loch Dunvegan, this castle has been the seat of the chiefs of the Clan MacLeod for over eight centuries. Its architecture is a unique mix of building styles due to the numerous renovations that took place over the years.

# 9 Skye Museum of Island Life
📍 Kilmuir ⏱ Easter–Sep: 10am–5pm Mon–Sat 🌐 skyemuseum.co.uk ↗
Discover what island life was like 100 years ago at this award-winning museum, which takes visitors back in time to an old Highland village comprising a small community of well-preserved thatched cottages and crofts.

## FLORA MACDONALD

"Bonnie Prince Charlie" was pursued relentlessly by government troops following his defeat at Culloden. He escaped to Skye disguised as a maidservant thanks to the courageous Flora MacDonald. She was imprisoned for this act. On her release she emigrated to America, but later returned to Skye, where she died in 1790. One of the prince's bedsheets was her burial shroud.

# 10 Talisker Distillery
🎫 For tours only 🌐 malts.com ↗ ↗
Overlooking the Black Cuillins from the pretty banks of Loch Harport at Carbost, Talisker is the oldest working distillery on the island. It is famed for its sweet, full-bodied Highland malts, which are often described as "the lava of the Cuillins".

**Talisker Distillery on Loch Harport**

# LOCH NESS AND THE GREAT GLEN

📍 E3–D4

Stretching from Fort William in the southwest to Inverness in the north, the Great Glen is a steep-sided, forested and mountainous valley home to a series of dark, mysterious lochs. The most famous of them all is Loch Ness, known for its ruined castle and legendary monster. Castles and forts abound, reminding us of the area's strategic importance and evoking a sense of nostalgia and intrigue.

## 1 Caledonian Canal

An outstanding feat of engineering by Thomas Telford, the 97-km- (60-mile-) long Caledonian Canal connects lochs Ness, Oich, Lochy and Linnhe. Watch boats glide past at Fort Augustus.

**Boats moored in the Caledonian Canal**

## 2 Urquhart Castle
🕐 Hours vary, check website 🌐 historic environment.scot 🔗
Situated on the edge of Loch Ness, these ruins were formerly one of Scotland's largest castles. A fine tower house still stands, and the views from the top are well worth the climb. The state-of-the-art visitor centre displays an array of medieval artifacts.

## 3 Loch Lochy
A path on this loch's northern shore is now part of the Great Glen Walk and cycleway. Look out for the wonderful Cia Aig waterfall on the road to Loch Arkaig.

## 4 Fort William
🌐 visitfortwilliam. co.uk
Close to Glencoe and at the foot of Britain's highest mountain, Ben Nevis (1,345 m / 4,413 ft), this seaside town provides an ideal base for walkers. Almost every direction offers enticing terrain and it now has a reputation as the outdoor capital of Britain, thanks to the range of mountain and

**Urquhart Castle on the Loch Ness shore**

> ### 🌸 EAT
> The Dores Inn *(thedoresinn.co.uk)*, a beautiful spot on Loch Ness's north-eastern bank, offers excellent food and drinks, with sweeping views of the loch.

watersports activities available nearby. The less active can scale Aonach Mor on the Nevis Range ski gondola or take the Jacobite Steam Train to Mallaig.

## 5 Loch Ness
🌐 lochness.com
Almost 230 m (750 ft) deep and 37 km (23 miles) long, Loch Ness is the country's largest waterbody. Flanked by mountains, castle and abbey ruins, and charming villages, Loch Ness is worthy of its fame. Jacobite lake cruises *(jacobite.co.uk)* start from the north road along its bank. Other cruises leave from Inverness.

## 6 Great Glen Water Park
🌐 greatglenwaterpark.co.uk
A sensitively landscaped centre among trees on Loch Oich, this water park offers spectacular views and activities. You can go canoeing, kayaking, canyoning, rock climbing or shoot the rapids on a raft.

## 7 Inverness
The "Capital of the Highlands", Inverness is a bustling shopping centre set below a pink Victorian castle. The battlefield of Culloden *(p119)* is nearby and the visitor centre there revives the history of this event.

## 8 Fort Augustus
Fort Augustus is a delightful village situated on Loch Ness. Take a stroll beside the canal and the loch shore to watch yachts and canal cruisers along the Great Glen.

## 9 Glen Affric
A lovely forest road leads to Glen Affric, a renowned beauty spot, which has one of

the largest ancient Caledonian pinewoods in the country. From here, you can take a two-day hike to the west coast.

## 10 Fort George
Built in the aftermath of Culloden on a sandy promontory in the Moray Firth, Fort George is the mightiest artillery fortification in Britain. It is still in use as a barracks today.

### TALES OF NESSIE

First recorded by St Aiden in the 7th century, "Nessie" pops up time and again. Despite many hoaxes and faked photographs, there's still a body of sonar and photographic evidence to support the existence of large creatures here, and scientific opinion remains open. To decide for yourself, visit one of the Loch Ness Monster information centres in Drumnadrochit, which present the evidence.

**Picturesque setting of Glen Affric**

# NORTH COAST 500

**D4** **northcoast500.com**

**Beginning and ending in Inverness, the North Coast 500 (NC500) is a 516-mile (830-km) road trip around Scotland's rugged northernmost reaches. On the way, you'll discover white-sand beaches, sweeping mountains, mist-cloaked sea lochs, hidden fishing villages and spectacular wildlife – in short, the very best that Scotland has to offer.**

---

**TRANSPORT**
Though most people drive the NC500, the route is popular with cyclists, and there are several cycle hire outfits in Inverness.

---

**1 Bealach na Bà**
The single-track road to Applecross is not for nervous drivers. Hairpin bends climb 626 m (2,054 ft) to Bealach na Bà (Pass of the Cattle), with awesome views en route.

**2 Torridon**
This epic wilderness inspired Westeros, the fantasy land in *Game of Thrones*. It's easy to imagine dragons wheeling above the bracken-cloaked hills and sea lochs – if you do spot a set of giant wings, it's likely a majestic white-tailed eagle.

**3 Inverewe Gardens**
Here, the UK's tallest eucalyptus trees, scarlet and purple Chinese rhododendrons, and Blue Nile lilies flourish in the mellow microclimate of one of Scotland's leading botanical gardens.

**4 Cape Wrath**
Jutting into the sea, mainland Britain's northwest tip is an awesome seascape of towering sea stacks and rugged cliffs, crowned by what may be Scotland's most spectacularly sited lighthouse.

**5 Kylesku Bridge**
An engineering triumph, this 275-m

*Clockwise from far left*
**A hillwalker on Beinn Alligin, Torridon; Timespan exhibit; misty sea stacks, Duncansby Head; Bealach Na Bà**

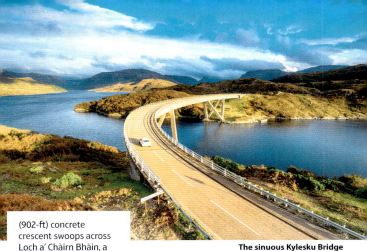

(902-ft) concrete crescent swoops across Loch a' Chàirn Bhàin, a long, narrow arm of the sea beneath hills where red deer roam.

**The sinuous Kylesku Bridge**

### 6 North Coast Beaches

The NC500 is studded with bays and coves that can look Caribbean on a sunny day. On the north coast, Torrisdale Bay is one of the best, with rolling combers that make it a magnet for surfers. You may even glimpse seals and otters.

### 7 Duncansby Head

Guillemots, kittiwakes and puffins nest on the wave-pounded cliffs and sea stacks here, overlooked by a pretty little lighthouse.

### 8 John O'Groats

Everyone knows that John O'Groats is the northernmost spot on the British mainland. Except it isn't: that honour goes to nearby Dunnet Head. Still, John O'Groats has its charms, including sweeping views across the Pentland Firth

to Orkney and dolphin-spotting boat trips.

### 9 Whaligoe Steps

Clamber (carefully) down the 330 steps that lead to a stunning natural harbour pounded by North Sea waves and hemmed in on three sides by cliffs that soar some 250 m (820 ft) above sea level.

### 10 Timespan

Helmsdale's Timespan centre recreates the ways of a 19th-century community founded by folk evicted from their ancestral

> **EAT**
> Just outside Wich, Puldagon Farm Shop and Restaurant (puldagonfarm.co.uk) is a great pit stop for a full Scottish breakfast, brunch or an afternoon snach.

homes by their landlord, the Duke of Sutherland (who preferred sheep to crofters). It also delves into the village's Viking roots and tells the story of Scotland's only gold rush, triggered by the finding of nuggets in the Helmsdale River in 1868.

# CULZEAN CASTLE

🅰 G3 🏰 Maybole ⏰ Castle: Apr–Oct: 10:30am–4:30pm daily (last adm: 4pm); grounds: Apr–Oct: 10am–5pm daily; Nov–Mar: 10am–4pm daily 🌐 nts.org.uk ♿

**Standing on a cliff's edge, this striking castle is one of the most magnificent in Scotland. First built as a simple keep in the 16th century, it was transformed by architect Robert Adam into a castle-mansion during the late 18th century. Today, its elegant interiors and extensive grounds are a delight to explore.**

**1 Country Park**
The castle's grounds became Scotland's first public country park in 1969. With a swathe of woodland, ponds, gardens and clifftop walks, this is widely regarded as the most magnificent park in Britain.

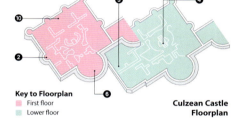

**Key to Floorplan**
🟥 First floor
🟩 Lower floor

**Culzean Castle Floorplan**

**2 Lord Cassilis' Rooms**
The late 18th-century rooms had Chinese-style wallpaper and a Chippendale bed.

**3 Armoury**
The Armoury houses a collection of 18th- and 19th-century weaponry purchased from the Tower of London. The fearsome arsenal includes a range of military swords and the largest collection of used flintlock pistols in Europe.

*Clockwise from top left*
**Firearm on display in the Armoury; Culzean's famed oval staircase; the elegant Camellia House**

## 4 Oval Staircase

The Oval Staircase, illuminated by over-arching skylight, is considered one of Adam's finest design achievements.

### TOP TIP

Don't miss the Walled Garden, where species of dessert grapes are grown.

## 5 Home Farm Visitor Centre

This is no ordinary farm, but more of a fortified village within the country park. It now houses a shop and a restaurant.

## 6 Round Drawing Room

Elegantly restored, this is the most beautiful room in the castle, with its circle of windows overlooking the sea.

## 7 Clifftop and Shoreline Trails

The views to the mountains of Arran are glorious from these trails. Two favourite destinations are Swan Pond and Happy Valley. Put on your walking boots and explore the glorious grounds.

## 8 Camellia House

Designed in 1818 by James Donaldson, a pupil of Robert Adam, this impressive Gothic greenhouse was originally built as an orangery. It is now used to grow camellias.

**Iconic turrets of Culzean Castle**

## 9 Eisenhower Apartment

The apartment on the top floor was a gift to the US president for his support in World War II. It is now a small hotel.

## 10 Long Drawing Room

Formerly the High Hall, this was the first room Adam transformed. It was restored in the 1970s.

### ROBERT ADAM

Born in Kinross-shire in 1728, Robert Adam was educated at Edinburgh University. His subsequent tour of Italy determined his Neo-Classical style, and he went on to set up an architectural practice in London, becoming the foremost designer of his day. A passionate worker, his fanaticism for detail was legendary. Adam died in 1792, the year Culzean was completed.

# THE CAIRNGORMS

D4–5  visitcairngorms.com

The highest mountain massif in the British Isles, the Cairngorms is made up of a magnificent range of peaks, wild lochs and ancient forests, and is home to a diverse array of wildlife, including red deer, golden eagles and mountain hare. In summer, the area is a popular spot for hiking and mountain biking, while in winter, skiers and snow-boarders take to its slopes.

## 1 Aviemore
visitaviemore.com

The gateway to the Cairngorms, the town of Aviemore is packed with visitors through the year. Aviemore has plenty of hotels, restaurants, pubs, cafés and shops along the main street stretching away from the train station.

> **TRANSPORT**
> The Strathspey Steam Railway *(stra thspeyrailway.co.uk)* runs from Aviemore to Broomhill, skirting the Cairngorms along the River Spey.

## 2 Loch Morlich
Surrounded by the Caledonian pines of Rothiemurchus Forest, Loch Morlich is a vast, tranquil lake at the base of the Cairngorms.

## 3 Speyside Wildlife
speysidewildlife.co.uk

A short drive from Aviemore, this place in the Caledonian pine forest is best for watching wildlife including badgers, pine martens and more.

## 4 Loch an Eilean
Loch an Eilean is a hidden gem, 8 km (5 miles) from Aviemore. Its crowning glory is an ivy-clad castle on an island. One of Scotland's best short walks is along this beautiful loch.

## 5 River Spey
Scotland's finest salmon river and birth-place of whisky, the Spey is a river of dark pools and fast rapids. It winds

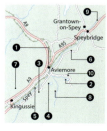

**Hiking in the pretty Cairngorms National Park**

 **DRINK** The Glenlivet Distillery, at the edge of the Cairngorms, offers tours giving an insight into how whisky is made, with tastings at the end.

grounds – the nest site is continually monitored to stop egg collectors.

## 7 Highland Folk Museum

🚩 Kingussie Rd 🕐 Jan–Aug & Nov–Dec: 10am–5pm daily; Sep & Oct: 10:30am–4pm daily 🌐 highlandhighlife.com

This open-air museum offers a cross-section of historical buildings – among them a church and a school – that have been moved here from their original location.

## 8 Glenfeshie

Nestled in the heart of the Cairngorms, this broad valley is a lovely spot for a walk. The area is home to some rare wildlife, so keep an eye out for ospreys, pine martens and eagles.

## 9 Malt Whisky Trail

🌐 maltwhiskytrail.com

Due to its climate and geology, Speyside is home to half of Scotland's whisky distilleries. The signposted "whisky trail" leads the way to seven of them.

## 10 Cairngorm Reindeer Centre

🚩 Glenmore 🌐 cairn gormreindeer.co.uk

Britain's only herd of wild reindeer was introduced to the Cairngorms in the 1960s. These charming animals, now numbering around 150, roam free.

through varied landscapes: moorland, forest, pasture and grain field.

## 6 RSPB Loch Garten Nature Centre

🌐 rspb.org.uk

Ospreys began breeding here in the late 1950s and each spring they return to Loch Garten from their wintering

*Clockwise from right* **Bridge across the River Spey; Highland Folk Museum; an osprey catching a fish; Loch Morlich and the snowcapped peaks of the Cairngorms**

# TOP 10 OF EVERYTHING

*Flowers in the Highlands*

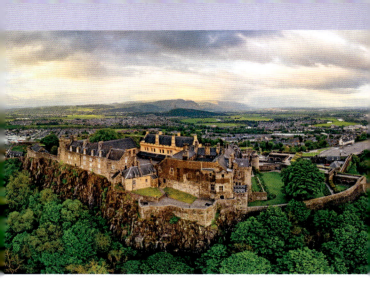

# CASTLES

## 1 Stirling Castle
Dramatically perched on crags overlooking the plains where some of Scotland's most decisive battles took place, this castle *(p107)* was one of the nation's greatest strongholds and a key player in its history. The gatehouse, Great Hall and the Renaissance Royal Palace are outstanding. Check out the castle's programme of special events, from tapestry weaving to sword fights.

## 2 Edinburgh Castle
The greatest castle *(p22)* in a land that's full of them, not only prized for its crowning position in the capital's heart, but also for its important history and the national treasures it holds.

## 3 Culzean Castle
Architect Robert Adam's masterful design and exquisite taste reached their apotheosis in this castle *(p40)*, which ranks as one of Britain's finest mansions. Set in a park, it commands a dramatic coastal view, looking seaward from the top of an Ayrshire cliff.

## 4 Caerlaverock Castle
A triangular ruin with immense towers, Caerlaverock *(p92)* still sits within a filled moat. Its history spans a siege by King Edward I in 1300 and a luxurious upgrade shortly before its fall in 1640. Its yellow sandstone walls glow beautifully pink and orange in the afternoon light.

## 5 Glamis Castle
This 17th-century fairy-tale castle *(p97)* is known for its literary associations: Duncan's Hall provided

**Magnificent Stirling Castle on a rocky crag**

the setting for the king's murder in Shakespeare's *Macbeth*. It also has a famous secret chamber and was the childhood home of the late Queen Mother. Rooms represent different periods of history and contain fine collections of armour, furnishings and tapestries. The gardens were laid out by 18th-century landscape gardener "Capability" Brown. Besides an Italian garden there are other green spaces, including a walled garden that features fountains, fruits and vegetables. There are nature trails as well.

**6 Balmoral**
Queen Victoria purchased the Balmoral Estate in 1852 and transformed the existing castle into this imposing mansion. Balmoral *(p114)* is still the private holiday home of the British royal family, and provides an insight into contemporary stately living.

**7 Blair Castle**
Seat of the Duke of Atholl, the only man in Britain still allowed a private army, this stately white castle *(p95)* is an arresting sight off the A9, the main road north. The oldest part dates from 1269, but after damage during the Jacobite campaigns Blair Castle was completely restyled and all the turrets added.

**Vintage furniture in a room at Blair Castle**

**Exploring the Eilean Donan Castle on Loch Duich**

**8 Eilean Donan Castle**
This is one of Scotland's most photographed castles *(p120)* due to its incredible setting – huddled on an island off the shores of Loch Duich and connected to the mainland by footbridge. The 13th-century stronghold of the Clan Macrae, it was left to ruin until its restoration in the 1930s.

**9 Dunnottar Castle**
A glorious ruin *(p12)* on a clifftop in Aberdeenshire with the sea crashing below, this is one of Scotland's most evocative sights. In the 17th century, the Scottish crown jewels were hidden here, away from Oliver Cromwell's marauding forces. Originally constructed for the Earl of Marischal in the 12th century, the surviving parts, mostly in ruins, date from the 15th and 16th centuries, and the 14th-century tower house is still in relatively good shape, though roofless. The most scenic way to arrive at the castle is by the coastal footpath from Stonehaven.

**10 Cawdor Castle**
Whether or not the real Macbeth lived here in the 11th century, Cawdor *(p114)* is the sort of make-believe castle that has come to life to satisfy all your Shakespearean expectations. The castle is utterly magical, with its original keep (1454), a drawbridge, ancient yew tree and an extensive collection of weapons. The garden and estate are equally enchanting; there's even a maze to get lost in.

# HIGHLAND TRADITIONS

### 1 Kilts and Tartans
Tartan patterned cloth was worn by Celtic peoples as early as the 3rd century CE, but the iconic Scottish kilt and clan tartans are modern creations. Traditional Highland dress was banned after the Jacobite rising of 1745. It was revived in 1822 with George IV's royal visit, when the king himself wore Highland dress. Since then more than 2,000 designs have been registered, and kilts have become ever more colourful.

### 2 Shinty
This sport makes football look dull. Similar to anarchic hockey, this fast-moving game is entertaining to watch and usually takes place during winter and spring.

### 3 Highland Games
This summer spectacle is packed with bagpipes, dancers and athletes, and forms an essential part of any visit. Most popular are the kilted strongmen in the "heavy events", which include hurling monstrous hammers as well as tossing a tree trunk.

### 4 Clootie Wells
Clootie Wells pre-date the coming of Christianity to Scotland. Celtic people like the Picts and Scots attributed healing properties to natural springs and revered them as the homes of benevolent spirits, believing (as some Scots still do) that tying a *cloot* (cloth) dipped in the holy spring to a nearby tree would cure an illness as the cloth mouldered. Once widespread, the two best-known surviving wells are at Munlochy, on the Black Isle, and in Culloden Forest, near Inverness.

### 5 Gaelic Language
Once spoken from Argyll and Perthshire to the far northwest and the Hebrides, Scottish Gaelic is now spoken by around only 60,000 people, almost all of whom live in the Western Isles. The last decade has seen something of a revival of the language thanks to the encouragement of both education and broadcasting authorities. You'll see road and station signs in Gaelic all over Scotland, even in southern regions where it was never spoken.

**Highland dancers in traditional kilts at an event**

**6 Scottish Dancing**
Vital features of any Highland Games are the kilted dancers competing on stage. Among the most common Highland dances are Sword Dances and the Highland Fling. While Highland dancers perform solo, Scottish country dancing is a group affair.

**7 Bagpipes**
No sound is more evocative of Scotland than that of bagpipes. The great Highland pipes are played by pipe and drum bands, and by individuals playing for competitions or dances.

**8 Curling**
This sport is one that the Scots excel at in the Winter Olympics. Heavy circular granite stones, with a flat base and a handle on top, are used.

**9 The Loonie Dook**
Only the brave dare a dip in Scotland's near-freezing North Sea for the annual New Year's Day "Loonie Dook". The first "Loonie Dook" took place in 1986, and has since spawned similar charity events at Portobello, St Andrew's and elsewhere.

**10 Ceilidhs**
Ceilidh ("cay-lee") is Gaelic for "a visit among friends", but has taken on the meaning of "a party". Sometimes it is a hall with a band where everyone dances, at other times it is a communal performance where people sing, dance or play an instrument. Fun is guaranteed whichever you attend.

**Tossing the caber at a Highland gathering**

## TOP 10
## INNOVATIVE SCOTS

**1. Elizabeth Blackwell (1707–1758)**
Botanist whose illustrated book *A Curious Herbal* was acclaimed as the first scientific guide to the medicinal plants of the Americas.

**2. James Hutton (1726–1797)**
Hutton's studies of geology led him to suggest that the world was vastly older than previously thought.

**3. James Watt (1736–1819)**
His development of the steam engine ushered in the Industrial Revolution.

**4. Robert Stevenson (1772–1850)**
This engineer oversaw the construction of the first modern lighthouses around Scotland's coasts and invented the flashing beacon.

**5. Mary Somerville (1780–1872)**
Dubbed as "the Queen of Science", she was one of the first female members of the Royal Astronomical Society.

**6. Robert Knox (1791–1862)**
A pioneering anatomist, Knox is infamous for his involvement with serial killers, who he paid to supply cadavers for his studies.

**7. James Young Simpson (1811–1870)**
He developed chloroform, the first effective anaesthetic for use in childbirth and surgery.

**8. Alexander G Bell (1847–1922)**
The father of the telephone patented his revolutionary device in 1876.

**9. Alexander Fleming (1881–1955)**
Fleming discovered penicillin, changing the face of modern medicine forever.

**10. John Logie Baird (1888–1946)**
Baird's "televisor", later to be known as the television, was first used for BBC broadcasts in the 1930s.

**Scottish polymath Mary Somerville**

# LOCHS

## 1 Loch Maree
☑ C3

You'll pass this loch if you visit Inverewe Gardens (p121). Wonderfully situated among imposing mountains, Loch Maree is a revered fishing location next to a nature reserve. Red deer have been known to swim out to the group of wooded islands in the centre and make temporary homes there.

## 2 Loch Katrine
☑ F4

Famous as the inspiration for Sir Walter Scott's poem *Lady of the Lake*, this loch is the pearl of the area known as the Trossachs. Now incorporated into the National Park with Loch Lomond, it is sheer tranquillity compared with the other's bustle. A boat tour here is highly recommended – the SS *Sir Walter Scott* has been doing the job for over a century.

## 3 Loch Trool
☑ H4

This enchanting loch lies within a forest, in a much overlooked corner of Scotland characterized by its stunning

**Camping on the shore of tranquil Loch Trool**

wilderness. The loch is bordered by walks, which form part of the long-distance Southern Upland Way (p56). At the eastern end there's a memorial to King Robert the Bruce, King of Scots from 1306 until his death in 1329.

## 4 Loch Awe
☑ F3

A long sliver of a loch, Awe twists through forested hills and is dotted with islets. The remarkable St Conan's Kirk (p110) stands near the north end of the loch, as do the magnificent ruins of the 13th-century Kilchurn Castle. Take the southern road for the best scenery, and don't be in a hurry.

## 5 Loch Tummel
☑ E4

This small loch, with its shimmering brilliance, was a favourite of Queen Victoria; stand at her preferred spot on the north side at Queen's View. The vista to the distant peak of Schiehallion (p55) is splendid, complemented in autumn by sweeps of colourful forest. Take the southern

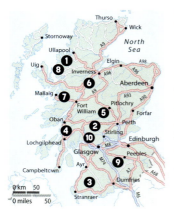

**Lush landscape of the spectacular Loch Lomond**

road to find the best picnic spots by the loch, and don't miss the river gorge walks at nearby Killiecrankie *(p98)*.

**6** **Loch Ness**
Probably Scotland's most famous loch *(p36)*, this deep body of water is a major draw for its scenic splendour of the Great Glen, Urquhart Castle and the as-yet-unexplained sightings of monster Nessie.

**7** **Loch Morar**
The rival to Loch Ness, Loch Morar *(p122)* is Scotland's deepest loch at over 300 m (1,000 ft), and has long had its own legend of a monster – Morag (apparently identical to Nessie). Morar is easy to get to but seldom visited because its shores are largely inaccessible to cars, which makes it all the more delightful for walking. Nearby are spectacular beaches, known as the White Sands of Morar.

**8** **Loch Torridon**
 D3
This magnificent sea loch is reminiscent of a Norwegian fjord. The wall of red sandstone mountains to its north attracts hill walkers, and from the summits you can see all the way from Cape Wrath *(p133)* to Ardnamurchan. A lovely one-way walk takes you from Diabeg to Inveralligin, with a series of refreshing *lochans* (small lochs) for swimming if the weather's hot.

**9** **Loch Skeen**
 G5
The hidden treasure at the end of an utterly magical walk, Loch Skeen is a tiny loch high up in moorland hills. The walk to it climbs steeply alongside the spectacular Grey Mare's Tail waterfall (note that it's dangerous to leave the path en route). The visitor centre, near the falls, shows a live feed of a peregrine falcon nest.

**10** **Loch Lomond**
The largest surface of fresh water in Scotland, Loch Lomond's *(p107)* beauty is celebrated in literature, song and legend. Forming part of Scotland's first National Park, in conjunction with the Trossachs, the loch is revered for its islands, lofty hills and shoreside leisure facilities.

# GARDENS

**1 Dawyck Botanic Garden**
📍 G5 🏠 Stobo, nr Peebles 🕐 Feb & Nov: 10am–4pm daily (last adm: 3:15pm); Mar–Oct: 10am–5pm daily (last adm: 4:15pm) 🌐 rbge.org.uk ⤴

An outpost of Edinburgh's Royal Botanic Garden, where trees are the speciality, this garden was started 300 years ago. With its enormous diversity and fine specimens, the garden is ideal for woodland walks. The visitor centre has a café, a shop and exhibitions.

**2 Kailzie Gardens**
📍 G5 🏠 Kailzie, nr Peebles 🕐 Apr–Oct: 10am–5pm daily; Nov–Mar: daylight hours daily 🌐 hailziegardens.com ⤴

This formal walled garden is an outstanding example of what was once more common on family estates. Marvellous roses fill the air with fragrance, and there's a pond stocked with trout for fishing.

**3 Botanic Gardens, Glasgow**
Positively bulging with greenery and colour, Glasgow's Botanic Gardens (p102) are a favourite with locals and visitors alike. The magnificent gardens date from 1817, and are particularly noted for their glasshouses. Foremost among these is the curved iron

framework of the restored Kibble Palace. An oasis of palm trees, ferns, orchids, begonias and many tropical species is found inside. Art exhibitions, theatre, festivals and plant shows also take place here.

**4 Royal Botanic Garden**
Edinburgh's prize garden (p82), founded in 1670 and moved to its current site in 1820, features huge trees, rock terraces and borders bursting with colour. The magnificent 19th-century glasshouses, with splendid collections of tropical and sub-tropical flora, are closed for a major restoration project intended to turn them into a pioneering zero-emission attraction. Watch out for special events, such as music, theatre and exhibitions of contemporary art.

**5 Inverewe Gardens**
A west coast phenomenon, these much-vaunted gardens (p121) are worth travelling a long way to see. The gardens were nurtured into

**Collection of orchids and ferns at the Kibble Palace**

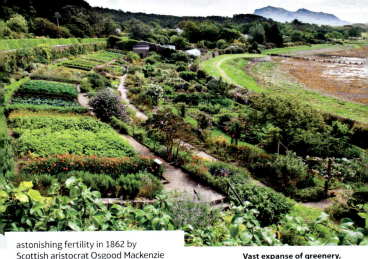

astonishing fertility in 1862 by Scottish aristocrat Osgood Mackenzie on his 8.5-sq-km (3-sq-mile) estate, and they became his life's work. Plants, shrubs and trees from all over the world form one of the finest botanical collections in the country, all in a stunning location on Loch Ewe.

**Vast expanse of greenery, Inverewe Gardens**

## 6 Logan Botanic Garden

🗺 H3 📍 Port Logan, south of Stranraer 🕐 Feb: 10am–4pm Sun; Mar–Oct: 10am–5pm daily; Nov: 10am–4pm daily 🌐 rbge.org.uk 🔗

The Logan has the largest number of sub-tropical species growing outdoors in Scotland. The palm trees and gunnera have grown to almost jungle proportions. Apart from the climate, there's a South Pacific feel to the place. It's usually much quieter than other gardens.

## 7 Crarae Gardens

Created in 1912 by Lady Grace Campbell, this Himalayan-style woodland garden (p108), overlooking Loch Fyne, has one of the country's most diverse collections of rhododendrons. Many of the seeds were gathered on private expeditions around the world and some species are now rare. In May the garden bursts into a mass of blooms. It is also home to the National Collection of southern beech trees. There is a waterfall, a gorge and several walking trails.

## 8 Arduaine Gardens

Overlooking the sea, this garden (p109) was established in 1898. It has another famous rhododendron collection, as well as blue poppies, giant Himalayan lilies, lush magnolias, camellias, tree ferns, water lilies and Chatham Island forget-me-nots. Having fallen into disrepair, Arduaine was lovingly restored by two brothers. See wildlife such as red squirrels in the woods, or spot seals and porpoises at the sea shore.

## 9 The Hydroponicum

A totally revolutionary place, the "garden of the future" (p122) has no soil but uses a clever water irrigation system to carry nutrients to the plants. Take a tour of the growing houses where they cultivate everything from tropical flowers to bananas. You can buy your own growing kits and fresh seasonal produce.

## 10 Pitmedden Garden

Originally laid out in a Classical French style in 1675 and destroyed by a fire in 1818, Pitmedden (p113) was meticulously recreated in the 1950s. The effect is stunning. Within a vast walled area are four elaborate floral parterres, three of which have heraldic designs.

# MUNROS

## 1 Ben Cruachan
**E3**

This set of seven peaks overlooks lochs Awe (p50) and Etive. The highest is 1,126 m (3,694 ft) and as this summit is considerably taller than any other mountain in the area, Ben Cruachan enjoys some of the most extensive views in the country. The name "Cruachan" comes from the war cry of the Campbell clan.

## 2 Ben Macdui
**D5**

Britain's second-highest mountain, at 1,309 m (4,295 ft), is best climbed from the Cairngorm ski car park. Reached by a high-altitude plateau covered in Arctic flora, it overlooks the magnificent Lairig Ghru, a deep rift dividing the Cairngorm range.

## 3 Ben Vorlich
**F4**

Uncomplicated Ben Vorlich, which overlooks Loch Earn, is perfect for anyone looking to bag their first Munro. Take the southern road and start from Ardvorlich. At the top, at 985 m (3,232 ft), the views to the Breadalbane mountains are glorious. After soaking it in and taking some panoramic snaps, it doesn't take long to get down for tea in St Fillans.

**Soaring Liathach looming over Loch Clair**

## 4 Liathach
**D3**

You could pick any of the famous Torridon mountains (p120) and guarantee not to be disappointed, but this is a particular beauty. A massive mound of red sandstone topped with white quartzite, Liathach has distinctive parallel bands of escarpments. At 1,055 m (3,461 ft), this is a relatively difficult and strenuous mountain to climb, but worth every bit of effort.

## 5 Ben Lomond
**F4**

Rising proudly from the wooded banks of its namesake loch, Ben Lomond's tall mass dominates the panorama. One of the smallest Munros at 973 m (3,192 ft), it has a well-used track, which is steep in places. There are tremendous views over the Loch Lomond and Trossachs National Park (p107). It is best to start at Rowardennan, where there's a hotel and hostel.

## 6 Ben Hope
**B4**

Ben Hope is the most northerly Munro, with its neighbour, Foinaven. Rising starkly from the woods and moorland around Loch Hope, it has clear views to

**WHAT IS A MUNRO?**

Any Scottish summit over 3,000 ft (approx. 900 m) is called a "Munro" after Sir Hugh Munro, who published a list of them in 1891. There are 282 Munros, and "Munro-bagging" is a popular pastime. Most can be walked safely without climbing skills, but it is vital to plan well and be properly equipped and competent in map-reading.

**Trekking towards the summit of Ben Nevis**

the Orkneys. The only difficulty in bagging this 927-m (3,040-ft) peak is the scree and rocky terrain, but this is a prestigious mountain to have underfoot.

# 7 The Five Sisters
☑ D3

This superb range of mountains has five prominent peaks towering above Glen Shiel in the West Highlands. Start at the highest part of the main road (A87) to save yourself an hour's climbing. Once you're on the summit ridge it's a long series of undulations, but worth it for fantastic views of the Cuillins on Skye (p34).

# 8 Buchaille Etive Mor
☑ E3

The 1,021-m- (3,350-ft-) tall "Great Shepherd of Etive" stands as guardian to the eastern entrance to Glencoe (p121). As an introduction to a place of legendary beauty, this wild mountain could not be improved. Approached from the southwest it can be climbed easily, but its magnificent crags demand respect.

# 9 Ben Nevis
Britain's highest mountain, Ben Nevis (p119) stands at 1,345 m (4,413 ft). A long path winds to the top. The summit is seldom clear of cloud, but if you strike it lucky you'll enjoy unsurpassed

views. In poor visibility take great care on the summit ridge as it's easy to lose the path, which borders a precipice.

# 10 Schiehallion
☑ E4

A much-loved mountain between lochs Tay and Rannoch, Schiehallion is most easily climbed from the pretty road connecting Aberfeldy with Tummel Bridge. It's an easy and rewarding Munro with which to launch your bagging campaign.

# WALKING ROUTES

## 1 Fife Coastal Path
📍 F5 🌐 fifecoastandcountry
sidetrust.co.uk/walks/fife-
coastal-path
This walk connects the famous
Forth and Tay bridges. It runs from
North Queensferry, near Deep Sea
World, to the small fishing villages
of the East Neuk such as Elie and
Anstruther, which huddle beside
rugged cliffs. The route then heads
north, through the historic town
and golfing capital of St Andrews.

## 2 West Highland Way
📍 E3–F4 🌐 westhighland
way.org
Connecting Fort William and Glasgow,
Scotland's first long-distance route
winds past the Nevis and Glencoe
ranges, crosses Rannoch Moor and
passes through some of the country's
most inspiring landscapes. The scenery
is stunning, though note the route runs
close to main roads at times.

## 3 Southern Upland Way
📍 H3–F6 🌐 dgtrails.org/
southern-upland-way
Britain's first official coast-to-
coast route is a wonderful mix
of mountain, moor, forest, loch
and pasture. It crosses the country
from Portpatrick in the west to
Cockburnspath in the east –
the preferred direction if you
want the wind at your back.

## 4 Great Glen Way
📍 D4–E3 🌐 highland.gov.
uk/greatglenway
This popular long-distance
route , connecting Fort William
and Inverness, probably packs in
more dramatic scenery per mile
than any other. The southern half
offers easier gradients along the
banks of lochs Lochy and Oich.
After Fort Augustus it climbs high
above Loch Ness – if that doesn't
take your breath away, the views will.

## 5 Speyside Way
📍 D4–C5 🌐 speysideway.org
Bordering one of Scotland's most
picturesque rivers, this path takes
you from the Cairngorms to Moray's
coast (with spurs to Dufftown and
Tomintoul). It is a walk full of interest,
with distilleries galore, bridges, stately
homes and a rich abundance of wildlife
to admire on the way.

## 6 Borders Abbeys Way
📍 G5–6 🌐 scotborders.gov.
uk/bordersabbeysway
Borders Abbeys Way is a circular
route that combines historical interest

**Hiking down the scenic
Fife Coastal Path**

with the irresistible appeal of the
gentle Borders landscape, with
its rounded hills, rivers and forests.
The track connects the four magnificent abbeys of Kelso, Melrose,
Dryburgh and Jedburgh.

## 7 Cateran Trail
🄿 E5 🅦 pkct.org/cateran-trail

The Caterans, brigands and rustlers
roamed this area in the Middle Ages.
Starting in Blairgowrie's soft-fruit hills,
this circular route wends to the wild
mountains of Glenshee, returning via
beautiful Glenisla, offering some of the
best of Perthshire. This is a quieter trail
than most.

## 8 Water of Leith Walkway
🄿 J5–K4 🅦 wateroflleith.org.
uk/walkway

From Balerno in the Pentland foot-
hills, on the outskirts of Edinburgh,
this urban walk follows the river
through wooded valleys and picturesque urban villages like Dean Village
and Stockbridge to meet the Firth
of Forth on The Shore in Leith. A
detour from Stockbridge through
the Royal Botanic Garden *(p82)* to
rejoin the walkway at Canonmills
is recommended. The route is well
signposted and can be easily explored
on foot or by bicycle.

## 9 Loch Lomond and Cowal Way
🄿 F3 🅦 lochlomondandcowalway.org

If you like things a little wilder, try
this one. The route is fully waymarked,
and passes through some of Scotland's
most varied landscapes (taking a good
map is essential). Start on the coast
west of Glasgow at Portavadie and
cross the hills of the Cowal peninsula
heading towards Inveruglas on the
stunning shores of Loch Lomond.

## 10 John Muir Way
🄿 F4–6 🅦 johnmuirway.org

This route runs coast to coast,
from Helensburgh in the west
to Dunbar in the east. It was named
for John Muir, father of America's
National Parks, who was born in
Dunbar. The trail passes through
spectacular mountains, sea coast,
national parks and canals.

**Strolling through the
verdant John Muir Way**

*Clockwise from top*
**Lush mountains
of Glencoe; a sign to
the West Highland
Way; hiking the
long-distance route**

# SCENIC JOURNEYS

Tweedbank, the Borders Railway is the longest railway line to be built in Britain for 100 years. Tweedbank station is a short walk from Abbotsford House, home of Sir Walter Scott.

## 4 The Road to the Isles
**D2–E3**
The A830 from Fort William to Mallaig is known as the "Road to the Isles". This is Bonnie Prince Charlie country and is crammed with Jacobite history. Driving it gives you the freedom to stop and explore sights, such as Glenfinnan, where Charles Edward Stuart placed his standard in 1745 and rallied the clans in his attempt to regain the crown; and Loch nan Uamh, from where he fled to France after being defeated at Culloden.

## 1 North Coast 500
The North Coast 500 (p38) is an 800-km (500-mile) circuit. From Inverness, the route goes west to Applecross then up the coast and along the tip of Scotland to John O'Groats, from where it heads back down to Inverness.

## 2 Take Flight
Soar over Loch Lomond or the Isle of Skye with Loch Lomond Seaplanes (lochlomondseaplanes.com). The seaplane offers spectacular views of Scotland's lochs and mountains. Tours should be booked ahead. Another exhilarating flight is from Glasgow to Barra with Loganair (loganair.co.uk). The island's runway is on a beach and disappears under the waves when the tide comes in.

## 5 Steam Back in Time
A trip "doon the watter" on the PS *Waverley*, the world's last seagoing paddle steamer, is a classic Scottish journey that all ages can enjoy. Launched in 1946 and originally fuelled by coal, the ship was saved from the breaker's yard in the 1970s and is now owned by a charity. Take a summer day trip from Glasgow to destinations

## 3 Borders Railway
**F5–G5  scotlandsrailway.com**
Opened in 2015 and stretching 56 km (35 miles) between Edinburgh and

**West Highland Line's Jacobite Steam Train**

such as Dunoon, Rothesay and Arran. Special excursions *(waverleyexcursions. co.uk)* run too.

## 6 Climb a Mountain

From the gentler slopes of the Eildon Hills in the Borders, to the mighty peak of Ben Nevis, Scotland's hills and mountains are wild, beautiful, challenging and irresistible. If you are not an experienced walker, or don't fancy going alone, rangers *(cairngormmountain.co.uk)* offer weekly guided walks around the Northern Corries of the Cairngorms.

## 7 Pedal a Trail

Whether you're a novice or an experienced biker, you're sure to find a trail to suit you in Scotland. There are demanding routes such as the Sligachan on Skye, a single-track circuit almost 45 km (28 miles) long. The 7 Stanes Centres *(forestry andland.gov.scot)*, in Dumfries and Galloway and the Borders, offer trails to suit all abilities. They have centres at Dalbeattie, Glentrool, Ae, Kirroughtree, Mabie, Glentress and Innerleithen and Newcastleton.

## 8 Bridge the Forth

🎫 F5 🌐 theforthbridges.org
When it opened in 1890, the Forth Bridge was the world's longest single-span cantilevered bridge, and it's still an iconic structure. Appreciate this Victorian marvel by taking the train across it, travelling from Edinburgh or South Queensferry into Fife. For that stunning upward shot of the vast framework of the Forth Rail Bridge, walk to Hawes Pier, and stand right under its massive supports at the east end of Edinburgh Road.

## 9 Ferry Crossing

A ferry-trip to a Scottish island is a wonderfully romantic experience. The main operator, Calmac *(calmac. co.uk)*, runs services to Arran, Skye and the Inner and Outer Hebrides. Ferries also run between Gourock and Dunoon and connect with trains from Glasgow Central. Scotland's last manually operated turntable ferry, the Skye Ferry *(skyeferry.co.uk)*, sails between Glenelg on the mainland and Kylerhea on Skye.

## 10 West Highland Line

The West Highland Line *(scotrail.co.uk)* runs from Glasgow to Mallaig. The journey takes around five hours and 30 minutes, and the train stops frequently, giving the chance to relax and enjoy the sights of Scotland's west coast. Look out for the Glenfinnan Viaduct, which featured in the Harry Potter films, as well as views of Ben Nevis and Loch Eilt. If you want to travel in style take the Jacobite Steam Train *(p120)*, which runs in summer.

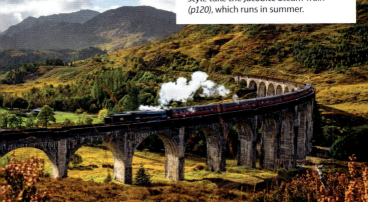

# ISLAND ATTRACTIONS

## 1 Fingal's Cave, Staffa
**⚐E2 Ⓦnts.org.uk**

An Uamh Binn, or Cave of Melody, Fingal's Cave is a spectacular sea cave on the uninhabited island of Staffa. Its giant hexagonal columns and mystical beauty inspired Mendelssohn's *Hebrides Overture*, and featured in a painting by J M W Turner. You can take a boat trip with Staffa Trips *(staffatrips.co.uk)* and see the island's fantastic wildlife such as basking sharks, seals and puffins.

## 2 Skara Brae, Orkney
The best-preserved group of prehistoric dwellings in Western Europe, this semi-subterranean village *(p134)* is 5,000 years old and pre-dates both Egypt's pyramids and Stonehenge. The nine houses were linked by covered passageways and you can see their "fitted" stone furniture. Artifacts such as gaming dice and jewellery are displayed in the visitor centre.

## 3 Jarlshof Prehistoric and Norse Settlement
**⚐B1 Ⓦhistoricenvironment.scot**

Overlooking the beautiful West Vow of Sumland is this historic settlement, first built over 4,000 years ago and in use until the 1600s. Highlights include oval-shaped Bronze Age houses and an Iron Age broch, as well as relics of Norse occupation, including Viking longhouses and outbuildings.

## 4 Islay's Distilleries
**⚐G2–F2 Ⓦislayinfo.com**

They say that Irish monks introduced distilling to Islay in the 14th century. At one time there were more than 20 distilleries on the island, producing its distinctive peat-smoked whisky. Now there are just nine, the most recent opened in 2018. The oldest, Bowmore, was first mentioned in 1779; the others are Ardbeg, Ardnahoe, Bruichladdich, Caol Ila, Bunnahbhain, Lagavulin, Laphroaig, and Kilchoman.

## 5 Iona Abbey and Nunnery
**⚐F2 Ⓦwelcometoiona.com**
**⚐**

Iona has been a centre of Christian worship since 563 CE, when St Columba founded his monastery here. It has been a pilgrimage site for hundreds of years. St Columba's shrine can

**The 8th-century St Martin's Cross, Iona Abbey**

**Hexagonal columns of basalt at Fingal's Cave**

be seen, as well as the 13th-century abbey church, and 8th-century stone crosses. Scottish kings and clan chiefs are said to be buried in the graveyard of the abbey.

# 6 Calanais Standing Stones, Lewis

📍 B2 🌐 historicenvironment.scot
These magnificent stones, arranged in a cross shape with a central circle, were erected around 5,000 years ago. Probably built as an astronomical observatory by a religious cult, they were abandoned around 1,000 years later. There's an informative exhibition in the visitor centre *(callanishvisitorcentre.co.uk)*.

# 7 Quiraing and the Old Man of Storr, Isle of Skye

📍 D2 🌐 isleofskye.com
Running down Skye's northernmost peninsula is the Quiraing, a basalt ridge that overlooks the sea. Rugged monoliths rise from here, with the tallest being the Old Man of Storr at 49 m (160 ft). It is the most impressive and also most accessible of these natural rock formations, reached from the main road between Portree and Staffin by the 3.8-km (2.6-mile) Storr Ascent walking trail.

# 8 Arran's Food Trail

📍 G3 🌐 taste-of-arran.co.uk
With dramatic mountain peaks, serene beaches, inland lochs and stunning scenery, Arran *(p130)* offers all the beauty of rural Scotland. It is also known for its wonderful selection of food and drink. Put together your own island food trail by checking out its local oatcakes, ice cream, haggis, black pudding, cheeses, chocolate, whisky, beer, smoked fish, preserves and *tablet* (a bit like fudge, only harder and sweeter).

# 9 Kinloch Castle, Rum

📍 D2 🌐 nature.scot
This grandiloquent mock-Tudor castle, with its crenellated red sandstone turrets and Doric-style temple, was built for John Bullough, the 19th-century Lancashire textile industry millionaire who bought the Isle of Rum as a private retreat in 1881. The retreat is owned by the heritage organization NatureScot, which runs occasional visits in summer.

# 10 The Italian Chapel, Orkney

📍 A5 🌐 orkney.com 🔗
Created from two Nissen huts by Domenico Chiocchetti and his fellow Italian prisoners of war between 1943 and 1944, this church is their memorial. Inside is trompe l'oeil brickwork and an altar made from scrap; painted glass windows depict St Francis of Assisi.

**Lovely frescoes inside the Italian Chapel**

# OFF THE BEATEN TRACK

## 1 The Old Forge, Inverie
📍 D3 🌐 theoldforge.co.uk

Threatened with closure, this much-loved pub – claimed to be the most remote in Britain and accessible only on foot or by boat – was saved by a community buyout in March 2022. The bar has a great range of cask ales, craft beers and malt whiskeys. Live music performances take place fortnightly on Sundays.

## 2 Knoydart
📍 D3 🌐 visitknoydart.co.uk

The most remote part of mainland Britain, this peninsula of rugged hills and glens lies in a time warp that's inaccessible by car. However, regular ferries from Mallaig provide access to the village of Inverie. Knoydart is a favourite destination for landscape photographers, which says much about its beauty.

The Old Forge, Britain's most remote pub

## 3 Sunset from Craig Mountain Bothy
📍 C3 🌐 mountainbothies.org.uk

Capture stunning sunsets from this simple, isolated cottage, which has five-star views over the sea to Skye and the Western Isles. Only accessible by foot, Craig is 5 km (3 miles) from Little Diabeg or 9 km (5 miles) from Red Point – and a lovely walk it is, too. You'll need to bring all provisions and a sleeping bag, and bear in mind there's no phone on site.

## 4 Walk from Loch Morar to Tarbet
📍 E3

For a walk and boat trip through sublime scenery, follow Britain's shortest river (half a mile) from Morar's silver sands to Tarbet. Tarred at first, the way turns into an undulating track, which wends to its destination at the lovely bay of Tarbet. You'll need to book the ferry (westernislecruises.co.uk) in advance and arrive by 3:30pm to catch the ferry back to Mallaig.

**Falls of Foyers thundering down the hillside**

## 5 Elie Chain Walk
📍 F5

As exciting as it is short, this 2.5-km (1.5-mile) cliff walk involves steep carved steps and chains bolted into rock to allow high-tide access between the coves. The best route is to walk west along the cliffs from the small town of Elie, descend to sea level at the tip of the headland, and then return along the chain walk. The chains are inaccessible for two hours at high tide, and are unnecessary at low tide.

## 6 Drive from Ullapool to Kylesku
📍 C3–B3

Scotland's most beautiful road is best driven in spring, when it's almost consumed by yellow-flowering whins, or in winter when surf erupts against the shore, or on a blue summer evening when Assynt's mountains assume the shape of absurd scribbles. The choice is yours. Take the A835 north from Ullapool, go west at Drumrunie, follow signs to Lochinver, then the B869 to Kylesku.

## 7 Falls of Foyers
📍 D4

Foyers' upper falls are impressive; the lower falls even more so, plunging a spectacular 62 m (200 ft). The white torrent gushes into a black bowl,

**Camping in Knoydart by Loch Hourn**

hollowed deep in the forest near Loch Ness, and the roar of the rushing water is as magnificent as the falls themselves.

## 8 St Kilda
🌐 nts.org.uk

Scotland's first World Heritage Site, this archipelago of monumental cliffs was, until 1930, inhabited by a highly individual community who lived off the islands' millions of seabirds. Such is St Kilda's isolation that it has its own subspecies of mouse, wren and sheep.

## 9 Sandwood Bay
📍 B3 📍 Nr Kinlochbervie

Said to be one of the most beautiful and remote beaches in Scotland, Sandwood Bay is a picturesque and rugged strip of pink sand flanked by lofty cliffs, dunes and guarded by Am Buachaille, an impressive sea-stack. Sandwood Bay, part of the Sanwood Estate managed by the John Muir Trust, is a good place to spot dolphins and other marine animals.

## 10 Regional Feis
🌐 feisean.org

A feis ("faysh") is a festival of Gaelic arts combined with workshops. Lasting several days, most take place in the Highlands and islands, with terrific performances and energetic dances.

# FAMILY ATTRACTIONS

## 1 Landmark Forest Adventure Park

📍 D4 🏠 Carrbridge, nr Aviemore
🕐 Hours vary, chech website
🌐 landmark park.co.uk ⤢

This play and adventure centre has treetop trails, climbing walls, a Lost Labyrinth maze and a handful of rides. The top attraction is the Dinosaur Kingdom, which features over 20 life-size animated models.

## 2 Our Dynamic Earth

Housed in a spiked tent, this electrifying exhibition (*p82*) is a mix of education and entertainment. You travel through all sorts of environments, from volcanic eruptions tothe Ice Ages. Stand on shaking floors, get caught in a tropical downpour, fly over prehistoric Scottish glaciers and come face to face with extinct dinosaurs. The exhibition also goes further, looking at our future and pondering the realities of climate change.

## 3 Museum of Childhood

📍 P3 🏠 42 High St, Edinburgh
🌐 edinburghmuseums.org.uk

A feast of nostalgia, with toys from the 18th to 21st centuries, this place is a real family attraction. It features everything – from teddy bears to Teletubbies, Meccano sets to snakes and ladders, comics to satchels and slates. Highlights include a wooden doll dating to around 1740, a tiny Steiff teddy bear which travelled out of Vienna in 1939 on the last Kinder-transport train and a doll's house with electric lighting.

## 4 M&D's Scotland's Theme Park

📍 F4 🏠 Motherwell 🕐 Hours vary, chech website 🌐 scotlandstheme park.com ⤢

Expect fun for all at this huge fairground. For older kids, check out the big wheel, free-fall machine, flying carpet, kamikaze whirligigs and the giant "500 tons of twisted fun" roller-coaster. For the younger ones there are water chutes and merry-go-rounds.

**Exhibit on climate change at
Our Dynamic Earth**

There's also Amazonia, an indoor
tropical rainforest.

**5 Kelburn Country Centre**
📍 F3 📍 Nr Largs 📍 Adventure
Park & Secret Forest: Apr–Oct:
10am–6pm daily; grounds: all
year 🌐 kelburnestate.com 🔗
The family estate of the Earls of
Glasgow doubles as an adventure park.
There's an indoor play barn and adventure play areas. The Secret Forest, a
highlight, is a winding trail dotted with
colourful attractions, including a fairy-
tale Gingerbread House.

**6 Glasgow Science Centre**
📍 Y3 📍 50 Pacific Quay, Glasgow
📍 Apr–Oct: 10am–5pm; Nov–Mar:
10am–3pm Wed–Fri, 10am–5pm Sat
& Sun 🌐 glasgowsciencecentre.org 🔗
Housed in a landmark building, three
floors of hands-on experiments puzzle
and delight with miraculous science.
There's an IMAX screen and the world's
first revolving tower.

**7 The Den & The Glen**
📍 D6 📍 Maryculter, nr Aberdeen
📍 9:30am–5:30pm daily (last adm:
4pm) 🌐 denandtheglen.co.uk 🔗
This family theme park has models
of nursery rhyme and storybook
characters for kids to explore and
enter make-believe worlds. Humpty
Dumpty, Pooh and Postman Pat are
among those present and there's a
good indoor play area too known
as the Den.

**8 Go Ape**
🌐 goape.co.uk
Enjoy zip-wiring and
treetop thrills in
Glentress Forest, near
Peebles; Crathes Castle
(p116), near Aberdeen

**Exploring the tree-top canopy
on a zipwire at Go Ape**

and Queen Elizabeth Forest Park,
near Loch Lomond – the last includes
a 400-m (1,300-ft) zip wire over a
27-m- (90-ft-) high waterfall.

**9 Murray Star Maze**
📍 E5 📍 Perth
Found in the grand wooded grounds
of Scone Palace, one of Scotland's great
stately homes (p96), this fun maze – laid
out in a star-shaped pattern around
a central fountain – will delight kids
of all ages. It is named in honour of the
palace's aristocratic owners, the Murray
family. The maze is made of cropped
green and copper beech trees, echoing
the Murray tartan.

**10 Scottish Seabird Centre**
📍 F5 📍 Harbour Terrace,
North Berwick 🌐 seabird.org
Zoom in on the wildlife of the Firth of
Forth islands (the Bass Rock, Craigleith,
Fidra and the Isle of May) using the
interactive live cameras without
disturbing them here. See gannets,
kittiwakes, razorbills, guillemots,
cormorants, puffins and, between
October and December, grey seals
with their pups. There have been
sightings of bottlenose dolphins,
porpoises and even whales. The
centre also offers boat trips to
the Bass Rock or Isle of May.

**Gannet on the Bass
Rock island**

# GOLF COURSES

## 1 St Andrews
⚲ F5 🆆 standrews.com

Every golfer dreams of playing here. There are seven courses, including the famous Old Course. It is recommended that you book months in advance or take your chance in the lottery for unreserved places held the day before. Try and fit in a visit to the Golf Museum too, which is home to 17,000 objects showing the history of golf from the Middle Ages to the present. The restaurant at the Old Course Hotel (*p99*) is excellent.

## 2 Carnoustie Championship Course
⚲ E5 🆆 carnoustiegolflinks.co.uk

A delightful course, the superb links and great character of Carnoustie have earned it a world-class reputation. You'll need to present your handicap certificate to play here and reserve your tee time in advance, but there are two other good links if you don't get on the main one. Saturdays can be busy throughout the year.

## 3 Gleneagles
⚲ F4 🆆 gleneagles.com

Another legendary group of courses, in beautiful moorland attached to a luxurious hotel. There are three championship courses, including the PGA Centenary that was designed by Jack Nicklaus, and the PGA National Academy, a nine-hole course, which is ideal for beginners. For on-site dining, look no further than the restaurant.

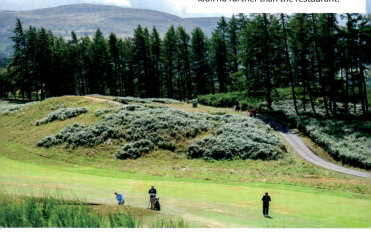

## 4 Gullane
**F5** **gullanegolfclub.co.uk**

Almost every blade of grass in this corner of East Lothian is dedicated to golf. Muirfield is the elite course but a private club. Gullane No. 1 is is one of the most scenic golf courses (handicap certificate is required to play here). Gullane Nos. 2 and 3 have no restrictions and can be accessed by anyone. If it is crowded, drive a short way to North Berwick, Haddington or Aberlady to seven more top courses.

## 5 Muirfield
**F5** **Gullane** **muirfield. org.uk**

This 18-hole championship course dates back to 1891, when it was first laid out by Tom Morris. Situated in lush East Lothian, by the pretty village of Gullane, it is home to the Honourable Company of Edinburgh Golfers. Visitors' days are Tuesday and Thursday. Availability of tee times can be checked in advance.

## 6 Troon
**G4**

Among the eight courses here there's one for everyone, from Fullarton's (golfsouthayrshire.com/ courses) fun course for beginners to the classics such as Darley and Portland. But the best is the Old Course (royaltroon.co.uk), a vintage Open venue. You need to apply well in advance.

## 7 Turnberry
**G3** **turnberry.co.uk**

Purchased by Donald Trump in 2014 and situated on the Ayrshire coast, the Ailsa Course has tested all the world's great players. A new 18-hole course, King Robert the Bruce, opened in 2017. With views of the iconic lighthouse, stunning coastline and ruins of the Turnberry

**One of the four courses at Gleneagles**

**Turnberry golf resort as seen from the Turnberry Hotel**

Castle, the course is particularly scenic. For expert tuition and a review of your game, contact the Golf Academy, a multi-million-pound addition to the hotel.

## 8 Old Prestwick
**G4** **prestwickgc.co.uk**

New courses come and steal the limelight but Old Prestwick glows as an enduring favourite. In 1860 it was the first venue to hold the British Open Championship. It remains a challenging course and one of Scotland's most venerated. It's usually very busy, especially on weekends.

## 9 Royal Dornoch
**C4** **royaldornoch.com**

This championship course has 18 pristine holes. It was laid out by Tom Morris in 1877 and follows the natural contours of the dunes around Dornoch Bay. It has a wonderful setting and feels less pressured than other quality links.

## 10 Nairn
**D4** **nairngolfclub.co.uk**

There are two championship courses here. The Nairn hosts major tournaments but also has a nine-hole course, the Cameron, for holiday golfers. Nairn Dunbar (nairndunbar.com) is the other top-notch course, with beautiful views to enjoy while playing your rounds.

# WHISKY DISTILLERIES

### 1 Macallan
📍 D5 🏠 Craigellachie
🕐 Easter–Sep: 9:30am–6pm
Mon–Sat; Oct–Easter: 9:30am–5pm
Mon–Fri 🌐 themacallan.com 🎫🅿️

Macallan is one of Speyside's most
famous brands, and the distillery
features one of the most modern
visitor centres in the valley. Aside
from a guided tour, you explore
whisky-making using the latest
interactive technology; become
a connoisseur by pre-arranging
an individually tutored nosing
and tasting tour.

### 2 Springbank
📍 G2 🏠 Campbeltown
🌐 springbank.scot 🎫🅿️

Campbeltown was once a
whisky smuggling centre,
and the Springbank distillery,
dating back to 1828, was built
on the site of an illicit still. This
independent, family-owned
business produces three distinctive malts – Springbank, Longrow
and Hazelburn – offering a choice
of tours and tastings.

### 3 Glenlivet
📍 D5 🏠 Ballindalloch 🕐 Mid-
Jan–Mar & Nov–Dec: 10am–4pm
Tue–Sat; Apr–Oct: 10am–4pm
daily 🔒 First two weeks in Jan
🌐 theglenlivet.com 🅿️

One of the first distilleries to be
legalized in 1824, remote Glenlivet
has been at the forefront of the
industry ever since. A comprehensive
tour includes the musty warehouse
where the whisky ages for 12 to
18 years; tastings are available.

**Whisky barrels at the
Macallan Distillery**

### 4 Laphroaig
🅟 G2 🏠 Nr Port Ellen, Islay
🆆 laphroaig.com 🔣🔣

With their heavy smoked-peat
flavour, the Islay malts really are
in a class of their own. This malt
is pronounced "la-froyg", but in
truth your pronunciation doesn't
matter – the taste is famous enough
for instant recognition. At the distillery expect a delightfully informal
and intimate tour with plenty of wit
in a fine sea-edge location.

### 5 Lagavulin
🅟 G2 🏠 Port Ellen, Islay
🆆 malts.com 🔣🔣

Like its rival Laphroaig, Lagavulin
whisky is a distinctive malt. It's
made in a traditional distillery
with unusual pear-shaped stills.
The tour is highly personal and
free of mass-market hustle.

### 6 Glenfarclas
🅟 D5 🏠 Ballindalloch 🅞 Oct–Mar
& Apr–Sep: Mon–Fri; Jul–Sep: Mon–
Sat 🆆 glenfarclas.com 🔣🔣

This distillery, established in 1836,
is owned and managed by the fifth
generation of the Grant family,
making it one of the few independent companies still going. A range
of tours are available: why not tour
the gleaming copper stills and then
finish off by taking a dram in the
splendid Ships Room.

### 7 Oban Distillery
🅟 E3 🏠 Stafford St, Oban
🅞 10am–5pm daily 🆆 obanwhisky.
com 🔣🔣

Established in 1794, this is one
of Scotland's smaller distilleries. It
produces a signature 14-year-old
malt, with a distinctive flavour and
scent, that owes more to the micro-

climate of the western mainland
than the peaty maritime malts of
nearby Islay and Jura. Tours include
the chance to sample three drams.

### 8 Highland Park
🅟 A5 🏠 Nr Kirkwall, Orkney
🅞 Apr–Oct: daily; Nov–Mar: Mon–Fri
🆆 highlandparkwhisky.com 🔣🔣

Found on Orkney, this rather remote
whisky distillery produces some
of Scotland's best whisky. The tour
here is excellent: prepare to be taken
through deep piles of malt drying
in a delicious reek of peat. The
facility has recently undergone a
major upgrade, helping to make it
one of Scotland's most environment
friendly distilleries.

### 9 Cardhu
🅟 D5 🏠 Knockando 🆆 malts.com
🔣🔣

One of the smaller distilleries, Cardhu
was proudly pioneered by a woman.
It produces a distinguished single
malt and provides the heart of the
Johnnie Walker blend. A range of tours
are available.

### 10 Talisker
🅟 D2 🆆 malts.com 🔣🔣

Skye's original distillery has been
producing a highly respected malt
since 1830. Lively, informative tours
last 40 minutes. Tours are organized
all through the year but are less
frequent in winter. Make sure to
book ahead in summer.

**Talisker Distillery, on the
Isle of Skye**

# LOCAL DISHES

**1 Haggis**
Scotland's national dish, served as the centrepiece of every Burns Night dinner, is made from the minced heart, liver, and lungs of a sheep, combined with oatmeal, suet and spices. There are also excellent veggie lentil-based versions. Haggis is usually served with mashed "neeps" (swede) and "tatties" (potatoes); for a gourmet take, try The Scran and Scallie in Edinburgh (p87).

**2 Scotch Broth**
This hearty, filling and richly flavoured soup is ideal for a winter's day. It's made from mutton or beef stock, with leftover snippets of meat, and thickened with pearl barley and vegetables such as carrots and leeks. Scotch broth is a soup-of-the-day favourite at the Glen Clova Hotel (p99) on the edge of the Cairngorms.

**3 Stornoway Black Pudding**
Black pudding is a type of blood sausage popular across northern Britain. Made only on the Isle of Lewis, the Stornoway version is the finest of them all, with oatmeal giving it a superior texture. It's an essential part of a full Scottish breakfast: while in Edinburgh set yourself up for the day at Contini (contini.com), where it's served alongside haggis, bacon, sausage and all the trimmings.

**4 Stovies**
Potatoes and onions are slow-cooked with beef dripping (fat) and leftover roast lamb or beef to make super-hearty and delicious stovies. Many Scots swear by the dish as a remedy for the effects of a night of overindulgence, so it's a popular New Year's Day treat. Teuchter's Landing, a cosy pub in Leith (teuchtersbar.com), serves stovies by the mug.

**5 Clootie Dumpling**
This rich suet pudding is made with morsels of dried fruit, flavoured with spices, tied into a muslin "cloot" (cloth) and steamed. Like haggis, it's a Burns Night favourite; fried in butter, a slice can also complement a hearty Scottish breakfast. Clootie dumplings are a famous menu staple at the Speyside Centre's restaurant in Grantown-on-Spey (speysidecentre.com).

**6 Forfar Bridie**
Hailing from the Angus town of Forfar, the bridie is Scotland's answer to the Cornish pasty: a horseshoe-shaped meat pie of minced beef, (sometimes) minced onions and seasoning, wrapped in either shortcrust or flaky pastry. It's often served – for an extra calorie hit – with chips and baked beans. McLaren Bakers in Forfar (mclarenbakers.co.uk) has been baking what may be the world's best bridies since 1893.

**7 Rumbledethumps**
Creamy mashed potato, cabbage and onion are the key ingredients of this hearty baked dish from the Scottish Borders. Its glorious name is said to derive from the noise made as the ingredients are bashed around the pot. Sample it, alongside other Borders favourites, at Seasons restaurant in Melrose (seasonsborders.co.uk).

**A toasted muffin with slices of haggis and black pudding, topped by an egg**

**Light yet indulgent cranachan,
a classic Scottish dessert**

## 8 Cranachan

Traditionally served to celebrate the berry harvest in August – but now a firm favourite at any special occasion – this delicious dessert is made from oats, fresh raspberries, heather honey, cream and whisky. Sample the finest cranachan at the Witchery by the Castle in Edinburgh (p87).

## 9 Venison

Scotland's deer population is booming, making venison – wild or farmed – its most sustainable meat. Low in fat, it's a healthy alternative to beef, too, and is equally versatile, whether served as steak or cut into collops (thin slices), in hearty casseroles, pies or burgers, or even cured as charcuterie. Stravaigin in Glasgow (p105) has imaginative ways with local venison, or try it as salami at the Taybank hotel in Dunkeld (p98).

## 10 Shortbread

Buttery and crumbly, Scotland's most famous baked good is made from just three ingredients: sugar, butter and flour. You'll find it in tartan tins all across the country but for a treat enjoy melt-in-the-mouth shortbread as part of the legendary afternoon tea at The Balmoral's Palm Court tearoom in Edinburgh (p148).

## TOP 10 SEAFOOD EATS

**1. Cullen Skink**
Originating in the cute fishing port of Cullen on the Moray coast, this Scots ancestor of chowder is made from smoked haddock, simmered in milk and thickened with potato.

**2. Kippers**
Butterflied or filleted herring are salted and oak-smoked to make this favourite breakfast dish, often served with a poached egg.

**3. Arbroath Smokie**
North Sea haddock, smoked on the bone in curing sheds, are a speciality of the Angus town of Arbroath.

**4. Smoked Salmon**
Smoking over oak lends a rich taste and deep pink colour to boneless, thin-sliced salmon that melts in the mouth. Choose wild salmon if you can.

**5. Scallops**
Meaty scallops are delicious pan-fried and served with black pudding. Make sure they are hand-dived, not dredged.

**6. Finnan Haddie**
Undyed and cold-smoked over green wood and peat, this delicate smoked haddock is the main ingredient of Cullen skink.

**7. Partan Bree**
A silky crab bisque, based on stock made with roasted crab shells, thickened with rice and cream and sometimes sweetened with a dash of sherry.

**8. Kedgeree**
Scottish cooks added flakes of smoked haddock to this Indian-inspired dish of rice, hard-boiled eggs and spices, sometimes eaten for breakfast.

**9. Oysters**
The plumpest, tastiest native oysters are farmed in the sea lochs of the west coast and around Orkney.

**10. Lobster**
Scotland's clear, cold waters are the perfect environment for lobsters to mature slowly and develop firm, intensely flavoured flesh. Best enjoyed simply grilled.

# SCOTLAND FOR FREE

**1 Top Museums**
All city museums in Glasgow and Edinburgh are free, so you won't have to pay to see many of the country's highlights, such as the National Museum of Scotland (p28), the Scottish National Gallery (p26) and Kelvingrove Art Gallery and Museum (p30).

**2 Free Festival**
There are more than 9,000 free comedy, cabaret, music, theatre and children's shows held each year, all run by the Free Fringe during the Edinburgh Festival Fringe (freefestival.co.uk). Audience members can make a donation at the end of a show if they wish. Some comedy clubs also run free shows thoughout the summer festivals, while the Royal Mile is packed with performers all summer long; they don't charge, but they do hope for a tip.

**3 Glorious Garden**
Entry is free to Glasgow's glorious Botanic Gardens (p102), which offer riverside walks and an arboretum, as well as stunning Victorian glasshouses, the most famous of which is the Kibble Palace. There are fascinating guided walks in the summer.

**4 Ancient Stones**
Evidence of Neolithic peoples can be found at Calanais Standing Stones on Lewis (p63) and Orkney's Ring of Brodgar (p136). The Picts also left some visible reminders of their presence, like the mysterious carved stones and crosses around Aberlemno, near Glamis.

**5 Wild at Heart**
Scotland's wildlife is rich and varied, and it doesn't have to cost you a penny to see it. St Abbs Head National Nature Reserve (nts.org.uk) offers the chance to spot seabirds such as guillemots and razorbills. At the Scottish Dolphin Centre (dolphincentre. whales.org) you can enjoy land-based dolphin watching.

**6 Seat of Power**
Scotland's increasingly powerful Parliament (p24) sits in a striking contemporary building at the foot of Edinburgh's Royal Mile. Book in advance for a free guided tour (parliament.scot), which lasts for an hour and includes details about the architecture as well as the history of the Scottish Parliament. You can book a free ticket to attend the First Minister's Question Time.

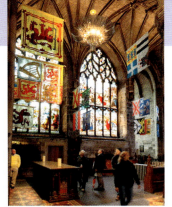

**Flags adorning the interior of
St Giles Cathedral**

# **7** Holy Orders
Most of Scotland's churches are free to visit, including the historic St Giles' Cathedral *(p24)* in Edinburgh and Glasgow Cathedral *(p101)*, though donations are welcome. Other churches include St Machar's Cathedral in Aberdeen.

# **8** Falkirk Wheel
Towering 35 m (115 ft) above the Forth and Clyde and Union canals *(p92)*, this eco-friendly engineering marvel needs a mere trickle of energy to lift vessels between the two waterways. Watch it for free from the canalside visitor centre.

# **9** Ancient Trees
Scotland is home to some mighty trees that you can see for free. The most famous are the Birnam Oak in Dunkeld *(p98)*, said to be the last survivor of Birnam Wood mentioned in *Macbeth*; and the 3,000-year-old Fortingall Yew in Fortingall's churchyard a short drive west of Pitlochry – a contender for Britain's oldest tree.

# **10** Salmon Leap
On the Tummel in Pitlochry *(p97)*, you can watch salmon leaping up the specially constructed fish ladder, which bypasses a hydroelectric power station. It allows thousands of fish to complete their annual migration (Apr–Oct).

**Modern exterior of the Scottish
Parliament building**

## TOP 10
## BUDGET TIPS

**1. Getting to the Isle**
Use the free road bridge rather than the ferry to reach Skye.

**2. Historic Scotland Explorer Passes**
ⓦ historicenvironment.scot
For five or fourteen days, these give free entry to over 70 properties.

**3. VAT Refund**
Non-EU visitors can reclaim the 20 per cent Value Added Tax (VAT) at participating stores.

**4. National Trust for Scotland**
ⓦ nts.org.uk
Membership provides free entry to over 100 properties.

**5. Spirit of Scotland Pass**
ⓦ scotrail.co.uk
A Spirit of Scotland Pass gives free travel on railways and many ferries.

**6. Cairngorms Golf Pass**
ⓦ visitcairngorms.com
A pass provides 30 per cent off green fees at any of 12 courses.

**7. Wild Camping**
ⓦ outdooraccess-scotland.scot
Camp in the wild for free almost anywhere in the Scottish countryside.

**8. Stay in a Bothy**
ⓦ mountainbothies.org.uk
Enjoy free, albeit simple accommodation maintained by The Mountain Bothies Association.

**9. Sandemans New Europe**
ⓦ neweuropetours.e
Sandemans offers free 2.5-hour walking tours of Edinburgh.

**10. Stay in a Hostel**
ⓦ hostellingscotland.org
Many of Hostelling Scotland's hostels offer en-suite accommodation as well as dorm bunks.

**Camping beside a loch**

# FESTIVALS AND EVENTS

## 1 Music Festivals

Scotland offers up a diverse mix of musical events. Celtic Connections *(celticconnections.com)*, held in the last two weeks of January, is the world's largest festival of Celtic music. The summer sees both Edinburgh and Glasgow host jazz festivals *(edinburghjazzfestival.com)*, while TRNSMT festival *(trnsmtfest.com)* on Glasgow Green welcomes big names like Stormzy and the Arctic Monkeys.

## 2 Sporting Events

The Six Nations Rugby Tournament *(sixnationsrugby.com)*, held in early spring, is the highlight of Scotland's sporting calendar. But there's plenty going on throughout the year, from Highland games such as the famous Braemar Gathering in September *(braemargathering.org)* to rural island surf festivals like the Tiree Wave Classic in March *(tireewaveclassic.co.uk)*.

## 3 Whisky Galore

May is Whisky Month, and whisky-themed events take place all over the country. The Spirit of Speyside Whisky Festival *(spiritof speyside.com)* is a great opportunity to take part in tours and tastings in iconic distilleries. The Highland Whisky Festival *(highlandwhisky festival.co.uk)* showcases eight distilleries on the North Coast 500.

## 4 Foodie Favourites

Scotland's summer food festivals champion local flavours. Sample Loch Fyne seafood, wild venison and over 200 ales at Fynefest *(fynefest.com)*. Celebrating East Coast produce is Inverurie's Taste of Grampian *(taste ofgrampian.co.uk)*, a one-day flavour-fest that's easily worth the trip. For celebrity chef spotting, don't miss the Foodies Festival *(foodiesfestival. com)* in Edinburgh.

## 5 On the Big Screen

The Edinburgh International Film Festival *(edfilmfest.org.uk)* is the biggest name on Scotland's film scene, but events take place all over the country. Highlights include Glasgow Film Festival *(glasgowfilm.org)*, Banff Mountain Film Festival *(banff-uk.com)* and Dundee's Discovery Film Festival *(dca.org.uk)*.

## 6 Island Culture

The Orkney islands celebrate their patron saint with the St Magnus International Festival *(stmagnusfestival. com)*. Coinciding with midsummer, events usually include at least one world premiere of either music or drama, and feature some of the world's best musicians. Skye's Fèis an Eilein *(seall.co.uk)* in early July celebrates culture and music.

**Band performing at the Celtic Connections festival**

**Performing at the Royal Edinburgh Military Tattoo parade**

## 7 Literary Events

Charlotte Square hosts the capital's summer showcase of bookish talent (*edbookfest.co.uk*). It features best-selling authors for readings, debates and book signings. Held at the end of September in Scotland's National Book Town, Wigtown Book Festival (*wigtownbookfestival.com*) may be small, but it packs a literary punch.

## 8 Royal Edinburgh Military Tattoo

Held every night during the month of August, the massive spectacle of the castle's Royal Edinburgh Military Tattoo parade (*edintattoo.co.uk*) is a swelling moment of national pride and vitality.

## 9 Edinburgh International Festival and Fringe

The greatest extravaganza of music, drama, dance and opera on the planet, the Edinburgh International Festival (*eif.co.uk*), which runs for the entirety of August, features the world's most prestigious performers, while the Fringe (*edfringe.com*) brings the unknown and the avant-garde to the city.

## 10 Hogmanay

No other nation in the world sees in the New Year with quite as much passion. Every Scottish town and city celebrates in their own way. Think all-night street parties, highland flings, pagan fire festivals or torchlight parades and, of course, plenty of fireworks.

## TOP 10 SCOTTISH SHINDIGS

**1. The Ba', Kirkwall**
Jan
Wild ball game and free-for-all played in the town's streets.

**2. Up Helly Aa**
Late Jan
An incredible fire festival in which residents dress as Vikings and burn a replica longboat.

**3. Borders Rugby Sevens**
Apr/May
In rugby's heartland, each border town takes a day as host.

**4. Burns An' A' That!**
Late May
Scotland's top musical talent celebrates Scottish culture at venues around Ayrshire.

**5. Royal Highland Show**
Jun
Over 150,000 people celebrate the biggest, best and most cultivated in the farming world in Edinburgh.

**6. Pride Edinburgh**
Mid-Jun
Scotland's national LGBTQ+ festival, with a march through the city.

**7. Edinburgh International Jazz & Blues Festival**
Jul
A rival to Glasgow's jazz event, this is the capital's own festival of live jazz, and soul performances.

**8. Speyfest**
Late Jul
Renowned and talented folk and traditional music performers gather at Fochabers.

**9. World Pipe Band Championships**
Mid-Aug
Astonishing sights and sounds as 3,000 pipers from around the world play on Glasgow Green.

**10. Hogmanay, Edinburgh**
Dec
Internationally famed, Hogmanay is hosted at venues, with live music and fireworks. The celebration is held throughout the city.

# AREA BY AREA

*The Western Highlands*

# EDINBURGH

Known as "the Athens of the North", the Scottish capital abounds with historical sights and cultural treasures. At its heart lies Edinburgh Castle and the nearby Royal Mile, a charming street that runs through the city's uniquely intact medieval quarter. Just north lies the greenery of Princes Street Gardens, home to the famed Scottish National Gallery, while to the south you'll find the National Museum, a repository of Scottish history. North of the historic centre is the Georgian New Town, filled with upscale shops, boutique hotels and restaurants, as well as lovely urban villages, such as Stockbridge and Leith, that have one-of-a-kind shops and cafés.

*For places to stay in this area, see p148*

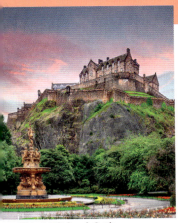

**Historic Edinburgh Castle atop Castle Rock**

# 1 Edinburgh Castle and the Royal Mile

This world-famous castle *(p22)* wears the nation's history. Here you'll find the Scottish Crown, Sword and Sceptre. The Royal Mile *(p24)* treads a straight but diverting path from the castle to Holyroodhouse.

# 2 Scottish National Gallery

Scotland's leading gallery *(p26)* includes masterpieces by the great Scottish artists, such as Raeburn and Ramsay, but is best known for its 15th- to 18th-century British and European paintings. In these collections, you'll find works by Botticelli, Velázquez, Raphael, Rembrandt, Rubens, Titian and many more besides.

# 3 Georgian House

⬛ L3 ⬛ 7 Charlotte Square ⬛ Apr–Oct: 10am–5pm daily; Nov–Mar: 11am–4pm daily ⬛ nts.org.uk ⬛

A restored mansion on Charlotte Square, this is the best place to start a walking tour of the New Town. The area was the first daring adventure into planned architecture at a time of sordid living conditions for the masses. Repainted in its original colours and furnished with antiques, it gives an insight into upper-class 18th-century Edinburgh. The beautifully proportioned buildings have lost none of their grandeur.

# 4 National Museum of Scotland

Two adjoining buildings *(p28)* in radically different styles and with very diverse contents present the nation's most treasured historical artifacts. It's worth visiting for the Lewis Chess Pieces alone, but don't expect to escape in under four hours.

**Statue, National Museum of Scotland**

National Monument for the dead of the Napoleonic Wars, the Nelson Monument, commemorating the Battle of Trafalgar and the Old City Observatory.

## 7 Royal Yacht Britannia

🔲 K5 🏛 Ocean Terminal, Leith ⏰ Apr–Oct: 9:30am–4:30pm daily; Nov–Mar: 10am–3:30pm daily 🌐 royalyachtbritannia.co.uk 🚹🎥

From 1953 to 1997 this was the British royal family's vessel. Wander the decks of this fabulous ship with an audio tour that tells of the life and times of *Britannia*.

## 8 Royal Botanic Garden

🔲 K5 🏛 20a Inverleith Row ⏰ Jan & Nov: 10am–4pm daily; Feb & Oct: 10am–5pm daily; Mar–Oct: 10am–6pm daily 🌐 rbge.org.uk

Scotland's premier garden *(p52)* with species from around the world. Lush greenhouses and glasshouses offer the perfect retreat on rainy days.

## 9 The Palace of Holyroodhouse

Originally the abbey guesthouse, this was turned into a royal palace *(p25)* by James IV of Scotland and is the monarch's official Scottish residence. The Queen's Gallery is lined with portraits of Scottish royalty. The Royal Apartments are associated with Mary, Queen of Scots. The monarch meets dignitaries in the State Apartments and the Throne Room is used for receptions and State occasions.

## PRINCES STREET GARDENS

An area of neutrality between New Town and Old, these lovely gardens shelter under the wing of the clifftop castle. During the festival they become a major events venue, and throughout summer the famous Floral Clock, comprising over 2,000 plants, blooms in a corner by The Mound. During Christmas, an ice rink is set up here, and there's also a festive market.

## 5 Our Dynamic Earth

🔲 R3 🏛 Holyrood Rd ⏰ Feb–Oct: 10am–5:30pm daily (Jul & Aug: to 6pm) 🌐 dynamicearth.co.uk 🎥

Every bit as exciting and illuminating for adults as it is for kids, Our Dynamic Earth *(p66)* takes you on a journey through time and tells the story of planet Earth, from the Big Bang to the present. Amid this rapid evolution, environmental concerns are brought to the fore.

## 6 Calton Hill

🔲 P2

Towering over the east end of Princes Street and rising above the New Town with fantastic views, Calton Hill is home to several Classical buildings: the

**Browsing artworks, Scottish National Gallery of Modern Art**

# 10 Scottish National Gallery of Modern Art

📍 J3 🏠 75 Belford Rd ⏰ 10am–5pm daily (Aug: to 6pm) 🌐 national galleries.org

Since it opened in 1960, this gallery has amassed some 5,000 works. Here you can find the work of diverse figures such as Picasso, Munch, Charles Rennie Mackintosh and the Pop Art trio of Richard Hamilton, David Hockney and Jake Tilson. The gallery itself occupies two buildings: Modern One, housed in a Neo-Classical building designed by William Burn in 1825, and Modern Two, just opposite, which hosts exhibitions.

**Impressive façade of the Palace of Holyroodhouse**

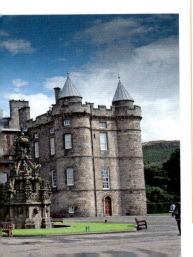

## A DAY IN EDINBURGH

### Morning

Start at the **Scottish National Gallery** (p26) at 10am. Ninety minutes should allow you to see the Botticelli, Canova and Raeburn's skating minister, the Rev Robert Walker and far more.

Enter **Princes Street Gardens** at the Floral Clock (opposite the gallery), and ascend the path to Edinburgh Castle (p22), taking care, as it's a steep climb.

Tour the castle and make sure you're present when the dramatic One O'Clock Gun goes off. At the **Redcoat Café** (edinburghcastle. scot), have a platter to restore your energy levels before soldiering on.

### Afternoon

Stroll down from the Castle Esplanade to the **Royal Mile** (p24), stopping off at the **St Giles' Cathedral** (p24) and probably several shops as well. Admire **John Knox's House** and have hot chocolate in **The Elephant House** (elephanthouse.biz) where the first of the Harry Potter books was written.

Turn right off the Royal Mile at Reid's Close (easy to miss) and visit **Our Dynamic Earth**.

If you still feel energetic, walk up the Salisbury Crags and **Arthur's Seat** for great views. Ninety minutes up and down or grab a taxi and be driven most of the way up.

# The Best of the Rest

**Signage on the exterior of the Writers' Museum**

## 1. The Writers' Museum
Celebrating three great Scottish writers, Burns, Scott and Stevenson, the Writers' Museum *(p24)* has rare books and items such as Burns's writing desk and Stevenson's wardrobe, made by the infamous Deacon Brodie, who was the inspiration behind *The Strange Case of Dr Jekyll and Mr Hyde*.

## 2. Scottish National Portrait Gallery
N2 Queen St nationalgalleries.org
Marvel at more than 3,000 portraits of famous Scots, including Robert Burns and Bonnie Prince Charlie.

## 3. St Giles' Cathedral
The Scottish Reformation was launched by John Knox in this church *(p24)*. Attractions include the Thistle Chapel and memorials to Robert Burns and R L Stevenson.

## 4. Greyfriars Kirk
N4 Greyfriars Pl greyfriarskirk.com
Historic church, best known for the grave of John Gray, owner of "Greyfriars Bobby" (1858–72), a devoted terrier who lived by his master's grave. A statue of this faithful dog stands outside the cemetery.

## 5. Surgeons' Hall Museums
P4 Nicolson St museum.rcsed.ac.uk
Appreciating Edinburgh's contribution to surgery, this group of three adjoining museums covers everything, including the history of pathology, midwifery and dentistry.

## 6. Hopetoun
J5 Sth Queensferry hopetoun.co.uk
This architectural gem built by Robert Adam, is both a stately home of the Earls of Hopetoun and an art treasury (paintings by Canaletto, Rubens, Rembrandt, to name but a few).

## 7. Real Mary King's Close
N3 2 Warriston's Cl, High St realmarykingsclose.com
Shiver as you tour this warren of streets hidden beneath the City Chambers. Closed off after the 1645 plague, they are said to be haunted.

## 8. Lauriston Castle
J4 Davidson's Mains edinburghmuseums.org.uk
This Edwardian mansion features a 16th-century tower house, lovely grounds, and fine furniture and antiques. Admission by tour only.

## 9. Scottish Mining Museum
L5 Newtongrange nationalminingmuseum.com
Don your headlamp for an enlightening underground tour.

## 10. Scotch Whisky Experience
M4 Castlehill scotchwhiskyexperience.co.uk
A replica distillery with the world's largest collection of Scotch whisky.

# Places to Shop

### 1. Edinburgh Books
**⚐ M4 ⌂ 145 West Port**
One of many independent bookshops, to the west of Grassmarket, sells new and second-hand books. West Port's selection focuses on the arts.

### 2. Hector Russell
**⚐ N3 ⌂ 137–141 High St**
Made-to-measure kilts and a gathering of the tartans. They offer kilts for hire too.

### 3. Armstrongs
**⚐ N4 ⌂ 81–83 Grassmarket**
A fabulous pre-loved clothing store that is filled with half a century's worth of vintage apparel and footwear. Find everything from velvet jackets to cowboy boots, kilts to dresses.

### 4. Halibut & Herring
**⚐ L6 ⌂ 108 Bruntsfield Place**
Find Scottish handmade soaps here and all manner of colourful, squeezy and bathroom accessories, in aquatic hues. It is a useful stop to buy gifts.

### 5. Edinburgh Printmakers
**⚐ L5 ⌂ Castle Mills, 1 Dundee St**
On display here are a range of limited-edition works from contemporary printmakers at reasonable prices.

### 6. I J Mellis
**⚐ N4 ⌂ 30A Victoria St**
I J Mellis's cheeses are celebrated all around Scotland, and feature in many Edinburgh menus, but the Victoria Street branch goes beyond, embracing a panoply of culinary deli-cacies. Stock your picnic hamper here.

### 7. Royal Mile Whiskies
**⚐ N4 ⌂ 379 High St**
This popular spot is favoured by whisky lovers from across the world. A cornucopia of all things alcoholic, particularly single malt Scotch whisky, it offers hundreds of varieties and regular tasting sessions.

### 8. St James Quarter
**⚐ P2 ⌂ Picardy Place/ Multrees Walk**
This vast multi-storey mall is filled with high-end clothing, jewellery and accessory brands, as well as countless bars, cafés and restaurants.

### 9. Edinburgh Farmers' Market
**⚐ L4 ⌂ Castle Terrace**
The city's weekly foodie fest spreads its wares beneath the castle crags every Saturday morning, selling everything from Scottish cheeses and venison sandwiches, to local craft beers and traditional Scottish sweets.

### 10. Tiso Edinburgh
**⚐ M3 ⌂ 123 Rose St**
An outdoor clothing and gear shop, Tiso Edinburgh has everything you need before heading for the hills. The Leith branch on Commercial Street also offers a café and a ski servicing centre.

**Artisanal cheese on display at the popular IJ Mellis**

# Bars and Pubs

### 1. Bow Bar
🔲 N4 🔲 80 West Bow St
Lush red and cream gloss paintwork envelops this modest pub, where the background sounds are the jovial chatter and clinking glasses.

### 2. The Blue Blazer
🔲 L5 🔲 2 Spittal St
Perfect for discerning drinkers, this place offers real ales and an array of malt whiskies. The back room hosts regular live folk-music sessions.

### 3. Bennet's
🔲 L6 🔲 8 Leven St
This classic old-school pub, with its ornate interior and superb portfolio of malt whiskies, real ales and fancy cocktails, is one of a vanishing breed.

### 4. The Dome
🔲 M2 🔲 14 George St
The Dome is a Corinthian-columned whale of a building, entered through a flight of steps flanked by nocturnal doormen. Its interiors are decorated with chandeliers and palm plants. There are many bars and dining areas such as the Georgian Tea Room and the majestic Grill Room. The Front Bar is great for cocktails.

### 5. BrewDog
🔲 N4 🔲 143 Cowgate
Scotland's most successful artisan brewery operates this industrial-chic altar to craft beer, a hugely popular oasis of real ales in the Old Town.

### 6. City Café
🔲 P4 🔲 19 Blair St
Ideally situated in the heart of the city's clubland, this popular bar packs in the capital's contingent of party people on weekend nights.

### 7. Bramble
🔲 M2 🔲 16a Queen St
Stone steps lead down to this maze-like, candlelit cellar where accomplished mixologists create some of Edinburgh's finest cocktails.

### 8. Café Royal Circle Bar
🔲 N2 🔲 19 West Register St
Walk in at lunchtime to swirling ceilings, brass lamps and a convivial atmosphere of both young and old, enjoying simple seafood dishes from the kitchen of the Oyster Bar next door.

### 9. Joseph Pearce
🔲 P1 🔲 23 Elm Row, Leith Walk
Swedish owners have taken this century-old Scottish pub and given it a Scandinavian makeover, creating a welcoming and family-friendly bar.

### 10. The Cumberland
🔲 M1 🔲 1–3 Cumberland St
Enjoy the well-lit, cosy interiors of this much-loved pub in the winter, or cool down in its side garden in the summer.

**Lavish interior of the bar at The Dome**

# Places to Eat

**Diners enjoying a meal at the Fishers in Leith**

## 1. Chez Jules
**M2  109 Hanover St  chezjules bistro.com · £**
This cheerful little bistro serves classic French dishes such as *moules frites* and *aioli* and beef bourguignon; the lunchtime set menu has terrific value.

## 2. The Witchery by the Castle
**M4  Castlehill  thewitchery.com · ££**
Aim for the Secret Garden room to experience The Witchery at its romantic best. It excels at dishes with a rural flavour. Try the foraged soup, roast wood pigeon, loin of venison.

## 3. Restaurant Martin Wishart
**K5  54 The Shore, Leith  restaurantmartinwishart.com · £££**
Make sure to book ahead for this Michelin-starred restaurant. The food is memorable and the lunch is of excellent value.

## 4. Timberyard
**M4  10 Lady Lawson St  timberyard.co · £££**
Originality is the watchword at this beautifully converted wood-working shop. The focus is on locally produced seafood, pork and game garnished with foraged ingredients, such as damsons and mustard leaf.

## 5. Fishers, Leith
**M2  1 The Shore, Leith  fishersrestaurants.co.uk · ££**
This seafood restaurant is loved for its honed cooking and warm ambience.

## 6. The Scran and Scallie
**K1  1 Comely Bank Rd  scranandscallie.com · ££**
This upscale gastro-pub, managed by star chef Tom Kitchin, serves modern classics based on Scottish produce.

## 7. The Kitchin
**F5  78 Commercial Quay  thekitchin.com · £££**
Sample exemplary French-influenced cuisine at Tom Kitchin's exceptional Michelin-starred restaurant.

## 8. Ondine
**N4  2 George IV Bridge  ondinerestaurant.co.uk · ££**
Seafood, from Scottish lobster to Portuguese prawns, graces the menu at this sleek and sophisticated restaurant.

## 9. The Little Chartroom
**K5  14 Bonnington Rd  thelittlechartroom.com · ££**
This tiny restaurant offers innovative dishes, such as octopus carpaccio and lamb with courgette and merguez.

## 10. Heron, Leith
**K5  87–91A Henderson St  heron.scot · ££**
Loacted on the Leith waterfront, Heron is surprisingly affordable for a Michelin-starred establishment. It offers a modern take on dishes, such as Orkney scallops and Arbroath smokies.

# SOUTHERN SCOTLAND

Bordered by England to the south and the firths of Clyde and Forth in the north, Southern Scotland is a bucolic region of rolling green farmland, purple-tinged upland moors and tranquil river valleys. Stately homes, palaces and castles lie dotted across the landscape, from regal Culzean Castle in the east to imposing Linlithgow Palace in the north. The region is also home to sites of religious importance, including the ruined abbeys of Melrose and Dryburgh, and the mysterious Rosslyn Chapel, found just south of Edinburgh. Elsewhere you'll find historic towns, national nature reserves and sights honouring famous Scots such as Robert Burns.

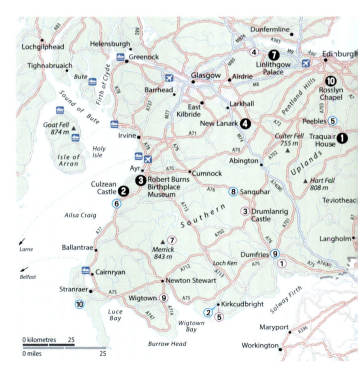

*For places to stay in this area, see p149*

Exterior of the lovely Traquair House

# 1 Traquair House
🅟 G5 🏠 Innerleithen ⏰ Hours vary, check website 🌐 traquair.co.uk ↗

Atmospheric Traquair dates back to 1107 and is Scotland's oldest inhabited house. The interior includes a hidden room leading to secret stairs along which Catholic priests could escape during persecutions. Both Mary, Queen of Scots and Bonnie Prince Charlie stayed here.

# 2 Culzean Castle
This cliff-edge castle (p40) was remodelled into a magnificent home for the Earls of Cassillis in 1777 by Georgian architectural master Robert Adam.

# 3 Robert Burns Birthplace Museum
🅟 G4 🏠 Murdoch's Lone, Alloway ⏰ 10am–5pm daily 🌐 nts.org.uk ↗

The world's finest collection of Burnsian memorabilia and manuscripts can be found in this museum. The cottage where the poet was born and spent the first seven years of his life is also nearby. The heritage park includes the Burns Monument and the Brig o'Doon bridge.

# 4 New Lanark
🅟 G4 🌐 newlanark.org ↗

In 1820, at the height of the Industrial Revolution, factory owner Robert Owen recognized the need for safe and efficient working conditions, matched by good-quality housing for his workers. New Lanark was the result, a modern industrial town that also comprised an education system and free healthcare. Now a UNESCO World Heritage Site, this living museum is still pioneering.

# 5 Manderston House
🅟 F6 🏠 Duns ⏰ Hours vary, check website 🌐 manderston.com ↗

This stunning and massive Edwardian mansion features a lake and woodland. It was built to impress Scottish society. The most lavish feature of the interior is the silver staircase; there are also fine artworks and antiques.

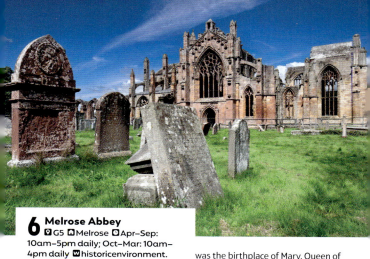

## 6 Melrose Abbey

📍G5 📍Melrose 🕐Apr–Sep:
10am–5pm daily; Oct–Mar: 10am–
4pm daily 🌐historicenvironment.
scot ⤢

Founded in 1136 by David I, this
was the first Cistercian monastery
in Scotland. It was rebuilt in the
1380s having suffered due to border
conflicts, but faced further damage
in the 16th century. What remains
of the abbey are the outlines of
the cloisters, the kitchen, monastic
buildings and the shell of the church.
An embalmed heart, found here in
1920, is probably that of Robert the
Bruce, the abbey's chief benefactor,
who had decreed that his heart be
taken on a crusade to the Holy Land.
It was returned here after its bearer,
Sir James Douglas, was killed in Spain.

## 7 Linlithgow Palace

📍F5 📍Linlithgow
🕐Apr–Sep: 9:30am–
5pm daily; Oct–Mar:
10am–4pm daily
🌐historicenviron
ment.scot ⤢

One of only four
royal palaces
in Scotland,
Linlithgow

**Statue at
Linlithgow
Palace**

was the birthplace of Mary, Queen of
Scots and provided a temporary safe
haven for Bonnie Prince Charlie during
the Jacobite Rebellion *(p10)*. Solid and
fortress-like on the banks of Linlithgow
Loch, the palace still looks majestic
in its semi-ruined state. This was
the finest building of its day, and
its master masons left a wealth
of carvings. Look around the Great
Hall and chapel and marvel at the
expertise of the crafters who laboured
upon this wonderful building.

## 8 Mellerstain House

📍G6 📍Gordon 🕐May–Sep:
12:30–5pm Fri–Mon 🌐mellerstain.
com ⤢

Scotland's most splendid Georgian
house (early 18th century) is another
creation by architect Robert Adam.
This vast edifice of perfect symmetry
on the outside has rooms of perfect
proportions within. The delicate
plasterwork of the library, resembling
fine china, is considered one of Adam's
greatest accomplishments. Exquisite
details abound throughout the interior,
while outside, grand terraced gardens
run down to an ornamental lake.

## 9 Dryburgh Abbey

📍G6 📍Nr St Boswells
🕐9:30am–5pm daily 🌐historic
environment.scot ⤢

Located on a bend in the River Tweed,
these are the most beautiful and

**Cemetry and ruins of the Melrose Abbey**

evocative ruins in southern Scotland. Founded in 1152, the abbey was destroyed by the English in 1322, 1344 and again in 1385, but each time it rose to magnificence once more, until it was finally consumed by fire in 1544. Despite having lain in ruin for 500 years, it is remarkably complete, and the quality of masonry is unbelievable. See it when shadows fall for the most spectacular views.

# 10 Rosslyn Chapel
🗺 F5 🚇 Rosslyn 🕐 9am–5pm daily (last adm: 3:40pm) 🌐 rosslynchapel.com 🔗

To the east of the A703, in the lee of the Pentland Hills, stands the ornate Rosslyn Chapel. Built in 1446, it has a great variety of styles and subjects. Most curious of all are the carvings of North American plants, which predate Columbus's transatlantic voyage by 100 years. The chapel has become extremely popular since featuring in *The Da Vinci Code,* Dan Brown's bestselling novel and the 2006 film adaptation of the same name.

**Beautiful stained-glass windows at the Rosslyn Chapel**

---

## A TOUR OF THE BORDERS

### Morning
Shop at the **Edinburgh Farmers' Market** or **I J Mellis** (*p85*) the day before your trip to make a gourmet picnic – as simple or as lavish as you like.

The next morning set off early and drive to **Rosslyn Chapel** to see the extraordinary carvings. Tear yourself away from this magical spot, and drive on to Penicuik and take the A703 to Peebles. It's worth having a break for coffee in this pretty town.

Now take the lovely Tweedside A72, then bear off onto the B7062 to reach **Traquair House** (*p89*). Explore this fascinating building, which is still home to the Maxwell-Stuart family, then enjoy lunch at one of the picnic tables in the extensive grounds.

### Afternoon
Return to the A72, then continue to visit either **Abbotsford House** (*p92*), the home of Sir Walter Scott, or drive a bit further to the romantic ruins of **Dryburgh Abbey**, where the great writer is buried. Both properties are a short drive from Scott's View, from where you can see the Eildon Hills while you delve once more into your picnic hamper for afternoon tea.

Return to Edinburgh for your evening meal, or continue to explore the Borders at your leisure and enjoy the stunning scenery.

# The Best of the Rest

### 1. Caerlaverock Castle
🅟 H5 🅟 13 km (8 miles) SE of Dumfries on the B725 🅟 Apr–Sep: 9:30am–5pm daily; Oct–Mar: 10am–4pm daily 🅦 historicenvironment.scot 🔗
Still remarkably complete, despite having been ruined for over 400 years, this moated triangular castle is a stunning sight.

### 2. Abbotsford House
🅟 G5 🅟 Nr Melrose 🅟 Mar & Nov: 10am–4pm daily; Apr–Oct: 10am–5pm daily 🅦 scottsabbotsford.com 🔗
Home of the great novelist Sir Walter Scott, filled with historical bric-a-brac.

### 3. Drumlanrig Castle
🅟 G4 🅟 Thornhill, Dumfries and Galloway 🅟 Castle: Easter, May bank hols. Jul & Aug: 11am–4pm daily; Grounds: Apr–Sep: 10am–5pm daily 🅦 drumlanrigcastle.co.uk 🔗
This 1676 castle, home to the Duke of Buccleuch, has a priceless collection of art and Jacobite treasures.

### 4. Falkirk Wheel
🅟 F4 🅟 Falkirk 🅟 Hours vary, check website 🅦 scottishcanals.co.uk 🔗
An engineering first, the world's only rotating boat lift was conceived with the intention of linking the Union and Forth and Clyde canals. Book a boat trip to soak in the views.

### 5. Kirkcudbright
🅟 H4 🅟 Dumfries and Galloway 🅦 kirkcudbright.town
Pronounced "kirkoobree", this fishing port and artists' colony offers a ruined castle, a gallery and arts centre, plus Broughton House, one time home of artist E A Cornel.

### 6. Scottish Seabird Centre
🅟 F5 🅟 North Berwick 🅟 Hours vary, check website 🅦 seabird.org 🔗
Remote cameras relay live action from the Bass Rock's 100,000 gannets. Take time for a boat trip.

### 7. Galloway Forest Park
🅟 H4 🅦 forestryandland.gov.scot
Area of superb loch, forest and hill scenery. Picnic at Bruce's Stone or have a day out on foot or on bikes.

### 8. St Abb's Head National Nature Reserve
🅟 F6 🅦 nts.org.uk
A national nature reserve on dramatic cliffs packed with birds. During the breeding season from May to June, it becomes an important site for more than 50,000 cliff-nesting seabirds. Don't miss the fishery museum in St Abb's village.

### 9. Wigtown
🅟 H4 🅦 wigtown-booktown.co.uk
Scotland's designated book town with many bookshops and a fantastic literary festival held each September.

### 10. Floors Castle
🅟 G6 🅟 Kelso 🅟 Jun–Sep: 11am–4pm daily 🅦 floorscastle.com 🔗
This magnificent property, built in 1721 for the first Duke of Roxburghe, is still the family home. Between October to March only the castle's grounds and gardens are open to the public.

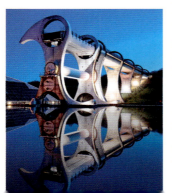

**Falkirk Wheel connecting the Union and Forth and Clyde Canals**

Elegant dining room at The Globe Inn

# Places to Eat

### 1. The Creel
📍F6 🏠25 Lamer St, Dunbar 🌐creel
restaurant.co.uk · ££
Local seafood dominates the menu at
this harbourside fine-dining restaurant.
Enjoy dishes such as East Lothian crab
with chilli, lime and cucumber gazpacho.

### 2. Castle Street Bistro
📍H4 🏠5 Castle St, Kirkcudbright
🌐castlestreetbistro.co.uk · ££
Cosy bistro offering Scots-French
influenced cuisine such as duck
breast with orange and cointreau.

### 3. Cobbles Inn
📍P1 🏠22 Rue du Grenier St-Lazare,
75003 🌐cobbleskelso.co.uk · €€
Popular gastropub offering bar lunches,
fine dining in the evening, and craft
beers from the Tempest microbrewery.

### 4. Wheatsheaf at Swinton
📍G6 🏠The Green, Swinton
🌐eatdrinkstaywheatshif.com · ££
Local lamb, fish and game are on the
menu at this country-style restaurant
with a lovely setting.

### 5. Peebles Hydro
📍G5 🏠Innerleithen Rd, Peebles
🌐peebleshydro.co.uk · ££
The changing menu at this restaurant
has dishes such as crusted cod loin
and desserts such as pear crumble.

### 6. Wildings Restaurant
📍G4 🏠Harbour Rd, Maidens,
Ayrshire 🌐wildingshotel.com · ££
An attractive seaside restaurant
with Isle of Arran views. The seasonal

menu features seafood, meat and
traditional Scottish dishes prepared
using local ingredients.

### 7. Marmions
📍G5 🏠5 Buccleuch St, Melrose 🌐mar
mionsbrasserie.co.uk 🕐Sun · ££
This French-style brasserie offers an à
la carte menu and wines for all tastes.

### 8. Blackaddie Country House Hotel
📍G4 🏠Sanquhar 🌐blackaddie
hotel.co.uk · £££
A classy restaurant serving Scottish
dishes made from quality local produce.

### 9. The Globe Inn
📍H5 🏠56 High St, Dumfries 🌐globe
inndumfries.co.uk · ££
Established in 1610, this gastropub
and restaurant was a favourite of poet
Robert Burns. The menu features dishes
such as rainbow trout escabeche and
roast partridge with red cabbage.

### 10. Knockinaam Lodge
📍H3 🏠Portpatrick 🌐knockinaam
lodge.com · £££
Sample traditional food with a modern
touch in a sumptuous country house.
A five-course tasting menu offers the
best of the kitchen.

# NORTH AND EAST OF EDINBURGH

Ranging from the Highland landscapes of Perthshire to the lush farmland of Fife, this area is one of Scotland's most diverse. Here, historic towns such as St Andrews – known as the "home of golf" – sit alongside modern, industrial cities like Dundee. Along the coast, meanwhile, lie a number of pretty fishing villages, including the artists' haunt of Crail and bustling Anstruther, known for its Scottish Fisheries Museum. There's regal history here in abundance, too: Fife's Falkland Palace was once occupied by Scotland's kings and queens, while Perth's fascinating museum now houses the Stone of Destiny, used to coronate royalty.

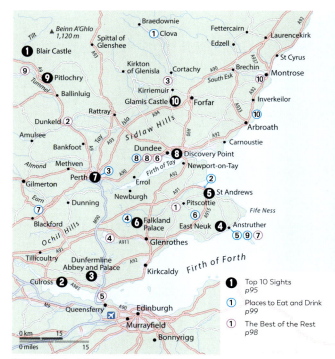

**1** Top 10 Sights
p95

**1** Places to Eat and Drink
p99

**1** The Best of the Rest
p98

*For places to stay in this area, see p149*

**The grand ballroom at Blair Castle**

# 1 Blair Castle

E4 Blair Atholl 10am–5pm daily atholl-estates.co.uk/blair-castle

This striking castle is the ancestral seat of the Duke of Atholl. Dating from 1269, it has been extended over the centuries and is embellished with crenellations, turrets and a grand ballroom. On the hour, one of the Highlander pipers plays in front of the castle.

# 2 Culross

F5 nts.org.uk

Once a thriving village, Culross prospered in the 16th century due to the growth of its coal and salt industries, most notably under the genius of Sir George Bruce. In 1932, the National Trust for Scotland (NTS) began restoring the town, and it is now a beautifully preserved 16th- and 17th-century village. The village is home to a 16th-century palace, a townhouse and an abbey. The NTS offers guided tours of the area from the visitor centre.

# 3 Dunfermline Abbey and Palace

F5 Dunfermline Apr–Sep: 9:30am–5:30pm daily; Oct–Mar: 10am–4pm Sat–Wed dunfermline abbey.com

Founded in the 11th century by Queen (later St) Margaret, the abbey's stunning feature is the 12th-century Romanesque nave. This was the burial place of Robert the Bruce – without his heart, which he requested be taken on a Crusade to the Holy Land. A skeleton with the heart chamber cut open was discovered in a grave here in 1818; the site is now marked by a plaque to honour the key figure of the Battle of Bannockburn (p9).

# 4 East Neuk

F5–6

*Neuk* is a Scots word for "corner", and the East Neuk refers to a small bend in the coastline along which is found a remarkable chain of picturesque fishing villages. They run from Earlsferry to Crail, and every one is a gem. Elie and Crail are probably the most quaint and are favoured haunts of artists. Pittenweem's beautiful harbour is still a working port, and Anstruther, a haven for yachts, has a bustling seafront. The latter is also home to the excellent Scottish Fisheries Museum (p98).

**Elie harbour as seen from the shoreline, East Neuk**

## 5 St Andrews
📍F5 🏛Cathedral & Castle:
Apr–Sep: 9:30am–5:30pm daily;
Oct–Mar: 10am–4pm daily
🌐standrews.com 🔗

The "home of golf" St Andrews has
the oldest university in Scotland, and
red-robed students add a colourful,
carefree atmosphere to this town.
St Andrews was once the ecclesiastical
capital of the country and its cathedral
is still a proud ruin. Its castle has unri-
valled examples of siege tunnels and a
curious "bottle dungeon". There's also
a long beach for walks, and plenty of
hip cafés and bistros.

## 6 Falkland Palace
📍F5 🏛Falkland 🏛Mar–May &
Sep–Oct: 11am–5pm Mon–Sat; Jun–
Aug: 10am–5pm Mon–Sat, noon–
5pm Sun 🌐nts.org.uk 🔗

A sense of history pervades this palace,
the home of Mary, Queen of Scots and
the Stuart kings from 1541. Restored

### HOME OF GOLF

The coastal links courses around
St Andrews are recognized as
the birthplace of golf – the
earliest record of the game
being played here dates to 1457.
Golfing heritage continues
in the city to this day, and
St Andrew's Royal and Ancient
Golf Club remains the ruling
arbiter of the game.

royal bedchambers and fine 17th-
century tapestries are on display. Most
intriguing is the oldest real tennis court
still in use in Britain, built in 1539. Unlike
the modern game, real tennis was
played indoors and is similar to squash.

## 7 Perth
📍E5 🌐perthcity.co.uk

Known as the "Fair City", Perth is
situated on the tree-lined River
Tay. Its streets are a delight of small
shops for browsing and its centre is
home to the Perth Museum *(perth
museum.co.uk)*, where the famous
Stone of Destiny – which monarchs
have been crowned on – is found.
North of the city, off the A93, is
the regal Scone Palace *(scone-palace.
co.uk)*, whose grounds contain the
Moot Hill, once the home of the Stone
of Destiny. The palace's annual events,
such as the Perth Highland Games
are quite the spectacle.

## 8 Discovery Point
📍E5 🏛Dundee 🏛Apr–Oct:
10am–6pm Mon–Sat, 11am–6pm
Sun; Nov–Mar: 10am–5pm Mon–
Sat, 11am–5pm Sun 🌐rrsdiscovery.
co.uk 🔗

The chill and hazards of Antarctic
exploration grip you in this hi-tech
exhibition. Focusing on the expeditions
of Shackleton and Scott, this display
uses original film footage, modern
images and interactive computer

**The picturesque university
town of St Andrews**

screens. Tour the Dundee-built
barque RSS *Discovery*, which carried
Scott on his first Antarctic expedition
in 1901. While in Dundee also visit the
Contemporary Arts Centre on Nethergate
for great exhibitions and its fine café-bar.

## 9 Pitlochry
📍 E4–5 📄 22 Atholl Rd
🌐 pitlochry.org

Surrounded by pine-forested hills,
Pitlochry has a long history of serving
visitors. Its proximity to Perthshire's
beauty spots and sporting estates was
the original draw, but now its major
attractions are a fine theatre and a fish
ladder, where salmon leap up a series
of pools to reach spawning grounds.
Above the ladder are lovely views of
Loch Faskally, popular with anglers.
Walking trails from here link with
the pretty gorge at Killiecrankie. The
Festival Theatre in Port-na-Craig has
shows all year.

## 10 Glamis Castle
📍 E5 📍 Glamis, Angus 🕐 10am–
4pm daily 🌐 glamis-castle.co.uk 🔗
The ancestral home of the Earls of
Strathmore since 1372, this magical
castle (p46) with towers, turrets
and treasures has a link with
Shakespeare's *Macbeth*.

**Medieval armour in the crypt at
Glamis Castle**

🕐

### AN EAST COAST DRIVE

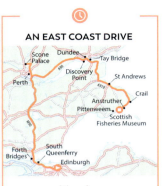

### Morning

Leave Edinburgh around 9am
and make for South Queensferry
to photograph the iconic **Forth
Bridges** *(p98)*. There's an
information centre where you can
find out about the history of the
bridges, and about the
Queensferry Crossing.

Cross the road bridge and take
the M90 to **Perth**. Stroll around
the town, then follow the A93
to **Scone Palace** to see where
Scottish monarchs were crowned.
If you're hungry, have lunch here.

Now it's about an hour's drive, via
the A90, to Dundee where you
can stop at **Discovery Point** and
shiver at the exploits of the
Antarctic explorers. Otherwise
cross the **Tay Bridge**, then join
the A919 to reach **St Andrews**, home
to Scotland's oldest university
and most famous golf course.

### Afternoon

You could easily spend the rest
of the day strolling around
St Andrews' streets, but if you
continue along the coast you'll
come to the East Neuk fishing
villages of Crail and Pittenweem
*(p95)* – not forgetting lovely
Anstruther, where you'll find the
**Scottish Fisheries Museum** *(p98)*.
Relax, soak up the scenery and
enjoy a meal in one of the
excellent fish restaurants *(p99)*.

**Forth Road Bridge with the Rail Bridge in the backdrop**

# The Best of the Rest

### 1. Hill of Tarvit Mansion
⚲ F5 ⌂ Cupar ⌂ House: Apr–Oct: 11am–4pm Sat & Sun; Grounds: 9am–dusk daily ⓦ nts.org.uk ⤢

This 17th-century mansion with vast grounds was remodelled in 1904 for a wealthy industrialist. It features cutting edge technology with electricity, telephones and central heating.

### 2. Dunkeld
⚲ E5

A village of great charm and character, with the noble ruins of its 14th-century cathedral and gorgeous riverside walks.

### 3. Kirriemuir and the Angus Glens
⚲ E5

J M Barrie, creator of Peter Pan, was born in Kirriemuir; his birthplace is now a museum. Nearby are the beautiful Angus Glens, great for scenic hikes.

### 4. Lochleven Castle
⚲ F5 ⌂ Kinross Pier ⓦ nts.org.uk ⤢

Sitting atop a tiny island in the middle of Loch Leven, this castle is one of Scotland's oldest. Mary, Queen of Scots was held captive here between 1567 and 1568. The loch provides a haven for birds. A 21-km (13-mile) heritage trail circles the loch, which is perfect for a scenic cycle or stroll.

### 5. Forth Bridges
⚲ F5

The iconic cantilever rail bridge, suspension road bridge and the striking Queensferry Crossing are best seen lit up at night.

### 6. V&A Dundee
⚲ E5 ⌂ 1 Riverside Esplanade, Dundee ⌂ 10am–5pm daily ⓦ vam.ac.uk

Standing above the Firth of Tay like the prow of a giant ship, the V&A Dundee showcases inspirational Scottish and international designs. It also has an excellent brasserie restaurant.

### 7. Scottish Fisheries Museum
⚲ F5 ⌂ Anstruther ⓦ scotfishmuseum.org ⤢

This museum offers a comprehensive overview of the history of fishing, with displays of boats, nets and more.

### 8. Verdant Works
⚲ E5 ⌂ Dundee ⓦ verdantworks.co.uk ⤢

Set in a refurbished mill, this is an invigorating presentation of the jute industry, the material upon which Dundee founded its urban economy.

### 9. Killiecrankie
⚲ E4–5 ⌂ Pitlochry

Known for its idyllic river gorge, this little village was the site of a famous Jacobite victory at the Battle of Killiecrankie in 1689. Visit the Soldier's Leap, where a fleeing Redcoat soldier is said to have jumped the 5-m (18-ft) gorge to escape the Jacobites.

### 10. Montrose Basin Wildlife Centre
⚲ E6 ⓦ scottishwildlifetrust.org.uk ⤢

Montrose's tidal basin is a hotspot for seafowl and waders. In winter, up to 80,000 pink-footed geese stop here during their migration.

# Places to Eat and Drink

**PRICE CATEGORIES**

For a three-course meal for one with half a bottle of wine (or equivalent meal), taxes and extra charges.

£ under £30  ££ £30–60  £££ over £60

## 1. Glen Clova Hotel

E5  Glen Clova, nr Kirriemuir  clova.com · ££

S tting at the end of a lovely glen, this hotel *(p149)* and restaurant has a simple all-day menu of staples including steaks and haddock, as well as vegetarian options such as veggie haggis burgers.

## 2. Old Course Hotel

F5  St Andrews  oldcoursehotel.co.uk · £££

For lovers of fine dining, the hotel's Road Hole Restaurant offers French-influenced cuisine, while the menu at Sands is more cosmopolitan, journeying from North Africa to Italy.

## 3. 63 Tay Street

E5  63 Tay St, Perth  D Sun & Mon  63taystreet.com · ££

This restaurant is the talk of the town, owing to chef Graeme Pallister. An extensive wine list complements a thrilling menu, which makes full use of Perthshire's prime natural larder.

## 4. Pillars of Hercules

F5  Strathmiglo Rd, Falkland  pillars.co.uk · £

A family-friendly café, this place offers delicious vegetarian soups, sandwiches as well as main meals.

## 5. The Cellar

F5  Anstruther, Fife  Sun–Tue  thecellarsanstruther.co.uk · £££

A seafood heaven, this restaurant is set off a courtyard behind the Fisheries Museum. Enjoy meat dishes, and some of the best fish in Scotland. Some dishes feature garlic shoots and sea buckthorn.

## 6. The Peat Inn

F5  Cupar  Sun & Mon  thepeatinn.co.uk · £££

Experience exceptional food and range of wine at the fairest prices, at this popular restaurant.

## 7. Andrew Fairlie

F4  Gleneagles Hotel  Sun  gleneagles.com · £££

Head to this two-Michelin-starred restaurant for terrific food.

## 8. Jute Café Bar

E5  Dundee Contemporary Arts Centre, 152 Nethergate, Dundee  jutecafebar.co.uk · ££

The cavernous interior at the Jute Café Bar is ultrahip. Enjoy a range of beers and innovative dishes at extremely reasonable prices.

## 9. Ship Inn

F5  Elie, Fife  shipinn.scot · ££

Seasonal food is served in a converted boathouse overlooking the village harbour. Vegetarian options are available.

## 10. The But 'n' Ben

E6  Auchmithie, nr Arbroath  thebutnben.com · ££

Within the white walls of this old fisher's cottage, seafood is the speciality, especially Arbroath Smokies *(p73)*. You'll also find good venison and local produce here.

**Exterior of the beautiful Glen Clova Hotel**

# GLASGOW

Straddling the River Clyde, Glasgow, Scotland's biggest city, buzzes with energy. A legacy of the 18th- and 19th-century mercantile and industrial revolutions, the centre is studded with several beautiful buildings, including the palatial City Chambers and impressive Kelvingrove Art Gallery and Museum. The latter is just one of many galleries that give Glasgow its cultural clout, with others including the House for an Art Lover and the Gallery of Modern Art. Other highlights focus on the history of Glasgow, with both the People's Palace and the Tenement House covering the lives of locals, while dotted across the city are plenty of places to eat, drink and be merry.

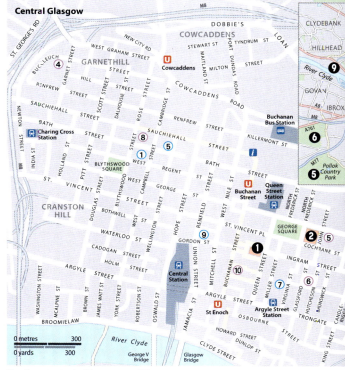

*For places to stay in this area, see p150*

**The Neo-Classical Gallery of Modern Art**

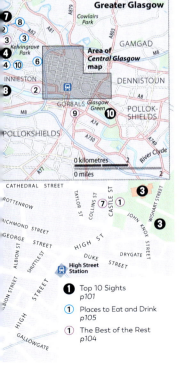

**Greater Glasgow**

## **1** Gallery of Modern Art

X4 Royal Exchange Square
10am–5pm Mon–Wed, 10am–8pm Thu, 11am–5pm Fri–Sun glasgow life.org.uk/museums

The four main galleries of Glasgow's Gallery of Modern Art showcase contemporary art and offer a consistently lively and thought-provoking programme of workshops and temporary exhibitions, featuring brilliant work by Scottish and international artists. In the basement is a sofa-adorned library with a café.

## **2** City Chambers

Y4 George Square For guided tour only at 10:30am & 2:30pm Mon–Fri glasgow.gov.uk

Designed by Scottish architect William Young in Italian Renaissance style, this is the finest seat of any council in Britain. The imposing building was opened in 1888 by Queen Victoria. Its elegant interior features Aberdeen granite, Carrara marble, mahogany, gold leaf, frescoes, mosaics, pillars and balustrades, showcasing the opulence of this building and making it the most impressive of its type in Scotland. The Banqueting Hall – with its murals, chandeliers and ornately patterned ceiling and carpet – does not fail to impress.

## **3** Glasgow Cathedral and Necropolis

Z3 Cathedral Square Apr–Sep: 9:30am–5:30pm Mon–Sat, 1–5:30pm Sun; Oct–Mar: 10am–4pm Mon–Sat, 1–4pm Sun

Immense and ancient, this cathedral was ranked by Pope Nicholas V in 1451 as equal in merit to Rome as a place of pilgrimage. Dedicated in 1136 and completed almost a century later, it has been in continuous use since then and has the original roof timbers. The choir screen is unique in Scotland, and the stained-glass windows are exceptional. On a hill to the east looms the Necropolis, a Victorian cemetery crowned by a monument to John Knox.

## 4 Kelvingrove Art Gallery and Museum

This world-famous museum *(p30)* is home to 22 fascinating galleries, whose exhibits span more than 5,000 years of human art and ingenuity, from Ancient Egypt to the 21st century.

## 5 Burrell Collection and Pollok House

Y3 Pollokshaws Rd 10am–5pm Mon–Thu & Sat, 11am–5pm Fri & Sun burrellcollection.co.uk

Sir William Burrell's (1861–1958) superb collection, housed in a purpose-designed building, has long been one of Glasgow's finest attractions. Highlights include beautifully crafted stained glass and Degas' evocative painting *The Red Ballet Skirts*. The nearby Pollok House gives a fascinating insight into Edwardian life and has Spanish paintings by Murillo, El Greco and Goya. There's a café in the original kitchen, and lovely walks in the surrounding parkland.

## 6 House for an Art Lover

Y3 Bellahouston Park, Dumbrech Rd 10am–4pm Mon–Fri, 10am–12:30pm Sat & Sun houseforanartlover.co.uk

In 1901 Glasgow's tour-de-force architect, Charles Rennie Mackintosh, and his artist wife, Margaret Macdonald, entered a magazine competition to design a "House for an Art Lover". It was to be "a grand house, thoroughly modern, fresh and innovative". Their exquisite vision remained just a design until 1989, when, precise to the smallest detail, the building and its contents were created. The café and shop are superb.

## 7 Botanic Gardens

Z2 730 Great Western Rd Gardens: 7am–dusk daily; Glass-houses: 10am–4:15pm daily (summer: to 6pm)

These gardens form a peaceful space in the heart of the city's West End, by the River Kelvin. The highlights are the glasshouses famous for their displays including palm trees, tropical orchids and ferns.

**Striking metallic dome, Glasgow Science Centre**

**8 Glasgow Science Centre**
The titanium-clad futuristic structures and dome of the Glasgow Science Centre *(p67)* are unmissable landmarks on the city's skyline. They are designed to mimic the hull of a ship, a homage to the Clyde's maritime and industrial heritage. Inside is a range of inspiring and innovative exhibits to fascinate visitors of all ages.

**9 Riverside Museum**
With acres of gleaming metalwork this museum *(p32)* has several hundreds of everything on wheels, including bicycles, cars, lorries, buses, trains and fire engines. Attractions include a series of recreated early 20th-century Glasgow streets and over 200 model ships illustrating the history of Clyde shipbuilding. Make sure you also visit the Tall Ship, moored outside. Built in the 19th century, it sailed around the world four times.

**10 People's Palace**
🗺 Z3 🚇 Glasgow Green 🔒 For restoration until 2027 🌐 glasgowlife. org.uk/museums
Typically Glaswegian, this is a museum of ordinary life. Nothing fancy or outstandingly old, but a fascinating insight into how the average family lived, worked and played in the not-so-distant past. There are prints, photos and films as well as an array of objects.

**Admiring the world-famous Burrell Collection**

### A FULL DAY IN GLASGOW

#### Morning
Take the subway to Kelvinhall station (or walk from the city centre) to visit **Kelvingrove Art Gallery and Museum**. Allow a couple of hours to explore and don't miss the Dutch Old Masters and French Impressionists.

Walk to the **Hunterian Art Gallery** *(p104)* to explore the **House for an Art Lover**, a reassemblage of the interiors of Charles Rennie Mackintosh's home. Tours start at 10am (11am on Sunday). Lunch at one of the many cafés on the nearby Byres Road or walk on to reach the **Botanic Gardens**, where you can picnic in the grounds or enjoy a meal in their tearoom. Stroll through the gardens and admire the orchids in the Kibble Palace glasshouse.

#### Afternoon
Take the subway to Cowcaddens station, from where it's a short walk to the **Tenement House** *(p104)*. This property is laid out much as it was when it was home to Agnes Toward in the early 20th century; it's a real slice of old Glasgow life.

Hop back on the subway to Buchanan Street station, where you can choose to walk down to elegant **Princes Square** *(p104)* to browse the shops, window displays, or make your way across George Square in time for the 2:30pm tour of the **City Chambers** *(p101)*. Have dinner at one of the city's many fine restaurants.

# The Best of the Rest

**The iconic Princes Square shopping centre**

### 1. St Mungo Museum of Religious Art
🅓 Z3 🅐 2 Castle St 🅦 glasgowlife.org.uk
Excellent overview of the world's religions through their art. The museum is illuminated by beautiful stained-glass windows.

### 2. Waverley Excursions
🅓 Z3 🅐 Anderston Quay 🅞 Jun–Aug 🅦 waverleyexcursions.co.uk
Travel back in time and experience the Firth of Clyde on the world's last seagoing paddle steamer.

### 3. Hunterian Art Gallery
🅓 Z2 🅐 82 Hillhead St, nr Kelvingrove Park 🅞 10am–5pm Tue–Sun 🅦 gla.ac.uk/hunterian
This gallery is best known for its collection of Rembrandts, its works by 19th-century American artist Whistler and the Mackintosh House.

### 4. Tenement House
🅓 W2 🅐 145 Buccleuch St 🅞 Jan–Feb: 10am–5pm Fri–Sun; Mar–Dec: 10am–5pm Thu–Mon 🅦 nts.org 🅕
Tenements were standard Glasgow flats and Agnes Toward lived an ordinary life in this one, now a museum, for over 50 years.

### 5. The Wonderwall
🅓 Y4 🅐 50 George St 🅞 24 hrs daily 🅦 citycentremuraltrail.co.uk
The huge mural highlights the achievements of the innovators and technologists of the University of Strathclyde.

### 6. Merchant City
🅓 Y4
East of George Square is this grid-plan of streets where the "Tobacco Lords" built their warehouses and mansions. The area is now full of designer shops and restaurants.

### 7. Provand's Lordship
🅓 Z3 🅐 3 Castle St 🅞 10am–5pm Tue–Thu & Sat, 11am–5pm Fri & Sun 🅦 glasgowlife.org.uk
Built as a canon house in 1471, this is the oldest surviving building in Glasgow, with a fine furniture collection and cloistered herb garden. Its low ceilings and wooden furniture create a vivid impression of life in a wealthy 15th-century household.

### 8. Mackintosh at the Willow
🅓 X3 🅐 215–217 Sauchiehall St 🅦 mackintoshatthewillow.com
Credited to renowned Glasgow designer Charles Rennie Mackintosh in 1903, this tearoom is also an exhibition centre.

### 9. Citizens Theatre
🅓 Z3 🅐 119 Gorbals St 🅦 citz.co.uk
An internationally famous venue; two modern studios complement the old Victorian auditorium.

### 10. Princes Square
🅓 X4 🅐 48 Buchanan St 🅦 princessquare.co.uk
Luxurious shopping centre in a renovated square of 1841 – the genteel atmosphere found here is heightened by the occasional appearance of a piano player.

# Places to Eat and Drink

### 1. Brian Maule at Chardon D'Or
📍X3 🏠176 West Regent St 🕐Sun & Mon 🌐brianmaule.com · £££
A true fine-dining experience that should not be missed. The chef, Brian Maule, combines the greatness of classic French cuisine with modern dishes that use top-quality Scottish produce.

### 2. Ubiquitous Chip
📍Y2 🏠12 Ashton Lane, off Byres Rd, Hillhead 🌐ubiquitouschip.co.uk · ££
Operating since 1971, and a champion of Scottish produce, this restaurant is Glasgow at its most endearing.

### 3. Stravaigin
📍Z2 🏠28 Gibson St, Hillhead 🌐stravaigin.co.uk · ££
A long-established restaurant where the house specialities include haggis and locally sourced seafood and meat.

### 4. Gloriosa
📍Y2 🏠1321 Argyle St, nr Kelvingrove Museum 🌐gloriosaglasgow.com · ££
Popular for its Mediterranean-inspired menu, this hangout also has wood-fired pizzas that are consistently excellent.

### 5. Sarti
📍X3 🏠121 Bath St 🌐sarti.co.uk · ££
A lively Italian restaurant, with a café and deli around the corner.

### 6. Chinaski's
📍Z2 🏠239 North St 🌐chinaskis. co.uk · £
A classy candle-lit bar offering a range of drinks and cocktails, complemented by good music.

### 7. Cup Merchant City
📍Y4 🏠4 Virginia Court 🌐cuptearooms.co.uk · ££
This delightful tearoom has pleasant courtyard seating and

**Elegant decor at the Ubiquitous Chip**

---

**PRICE CATEGORIES**

For a three-course meal for one with half a bottle of wine (or equivalent meal), taxes and extra charges.

**£** under £30 **££** £30–60 **£££** over £60

---

offers a wide range of afternoon menus, including gluten free, vegetarian and vegan options.

### 8. Cail Bruich
📍U1 🏠725 Great Western Rd 🕐Sun & Mon 🌐cailbruich.co.uk· £££
Helmed by Lorna McNee, Scotland's only female Michelin-starred chef, this is arguably Glasgow's finest fine-dining experience. Try the outstanding seven-course tasting menu.

### 9. The Horse Shoe Bar
📍X4 🏠17 Drury St 🌐horseshoe barglasgow.co.uk · £
Few pubs deserve to be considered a Glasgow institution more than this gem of a place. Friendly and economical, it is a cracking pub in which to soak up the city's ambience.

### 10. Mother India
📍Z2 🏠28 Westminster Terrace, Sauchiehall St 🌐motherindia.co.uk · ££
This restaurant is a must-visit destination for gourmands of all stripes. You'll find exquisite modern Indian food here.

# NORTH AND WEST OF GLASGOW

Encompassing wild uplands and tamer lowlands, this bucolic region became the focus of Scotland's first tourist industry in early Victorian times. With Loch Lomond and the Trossachs National Park at its centre offering a range of outdoor activities and experiences, that allure remains as strong today. In the west are the rocky peaks of the Isle of Arran and a seaboard of fjord-like lochs, where a mild climate supports some grand gardens. In the east stands Stirling, a key city in the country's warring past. Overlooking the plains where some of Scotland's most decisive battles took place, Stirling Castle was one of the nation's greatest strongholds. Here, William Wallace and Robert the Bruce fought for independence, a battle eventually won within sight of the castle on the field of Bannockburn.

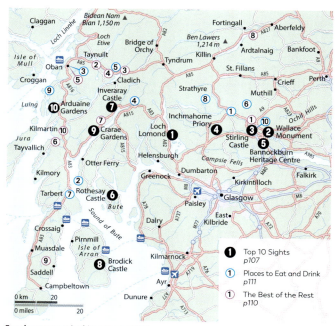

| | |
|---|---|
| **1** | Top 10 Sights *p107* |
| **1** | Places to Eat and Drink *p111* |
| **1** | The Best of the Rest *p110* |

*For places to stay in this area, see p150*

# 1 Loch Lomond and the Trossachs National Park

☑ F4 ☐ West Dunbartonshire, Argyll & Bute, Trossachs ☑ lochlomond-trossachs.org

Of Scotland's many lochs, Loch Lomond is perhaps the most popular and best loved. The Trossachs, designated as Scotland's first national park, is home to a variety of wildlife. This beautiful region of craggy peaks, sparkling lochs and scenic waterfalls is where the Lowlands and the Highlands meet. Luss is the prettiest village in the area, possessing a lovely sandy beach and some excellent restaurants. Cruises run from here, and from Balloch, Tarbet and Balmaha.

Boats on the calm waters of Loch Lomond

# 2 Wallace Monument

☑ F4 ☐ Apr–Oct: 9:30am–5pm daily (Jul & Aug: to 6pm); Nov–Mar: 10am–4pm daily ☑ national wallacemonument.com

Erected in 1869, this 75-m (250-ft) tower commemorates William Wallace and his fight for Scotland's independence. The climb takes you past Wallace's two-handed broadsword, while a hologram-style display shows a disembodied "talking head" (meant to represent Wallace himself after decapitation) that recites his pre-execution defence speech.

# 3 Stirling Castle

☑ F4 ☐ Apr–Sep: 9:30am–6pm daily; Oct–Mar: 9:30am–5pm daily ☑ stirlingcastle.scot

This magnificent castle (p46), which dominated Scottish history for centuries, remains one of the finest examples of Renaissance architecture in the country.

# 4 Inchmahome Priory

☑ F4 ☐ Hours vary, check website ☑ historicenvironment.scot

The Lake of Menteith is Scotland's only lake (as opposed to loch), and famed for the graceful ruined priory on the island of Inchmahome. It's in this beautiful spot that the infant Mary, Queen of Scots was looked after by Augustinian monks before she was spirited away to France.

# 5 Battle of Bannockburn Experience

☑ F4 ☐ Site: open all year; Heritage Centre: Feb–Dec: 10am–5pm daily ☑ nts.org.uk

The site of the decisive battle (p9) in 1314 is marked by a visitor centre and an equestrian statue of Robert the Bruce. Kids can try on helmets and view Bruce's cave to watch the fabled spider who inspired him to renew his fight.

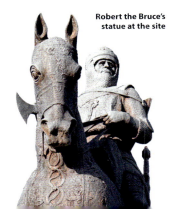

Robert the Bruce's statue at the site

**Rhododendrons in bloom at the Crarae Gardens**

## 6 Rothesay Castle, Bute

⬛ F3 ⬛ Castle Hill St, Rothesay ⬛ Mar: 10am–4pm Sat–Wed; Apr–Sep: 9:30am–5pm daily ⬛ historic environment.scot 🔗

By virtue of its age, design and deep-water moat (one of only two remaining in Scotland), this is a remarkable medieval castle. Built around 1200 as a defence against Norwegian raiders, it was restyled in the 13th century and fitted with high curtain walls and drum towers. Its circular courtyard is a curious feature and unique in Scotland. Bute itself is a mere 35-minute crossing from Wemyss Bay – north of Largs on the A78 – to Rothesay Bay; an even shorter crossing is from Colintraive to Rhubodach, on the north coast of the island.

## 7 Inveraray Castle

⬛ F3 ⬛ Inveraray, Argyll & Bute ⬛ Apr–Oct: 10am–5pm Thu–Mon ⬛ inveraray-castle.com 🔗

Despite the ravages of fire, Clan Campbell's family seat is a splendid pseudo-Gothic palace with pointed towers. It was built for the Duke of Argyll in 1745. The interiors were designed by Robert Mylne and contain Regency furniture and

priceless works of art. The Armoury Hall was stocked to fight the Jacobites. There's a hilltop folly in the grounds. The castle grounds host the Inveraray Highland Games, a colourful celebration of Highland culture.

## 8 Brodick Castle, Arran

⬛ G3 ⬛ Brodich ⬛ Apr–Oct: 10:30am–5pm daily ⬛ nts.org.uk 🔗

Originally a Viking keep, before the Dukes of Hamilton claimed it, this 13th-century fortified tower was extended by Oliver Cromwell and then transformed into a stately home in Victorian times. The last Hamilton moved out only in 1957. A solid red sandstone building with fanciful trimmings, it contains a noted collection of silver, porcelain and paintings. The gardens are beautifully maintained as are the woodland trails. The main ferry to Arran (just under an hour) is from Ardrossan, on the mainland coast, just north of Irvine.

## 9 Crarae Gardens

⬛ F3 ⬛ Nr Inveraray ⬛ Apr–Oct: 10am–5pm daily; Nov–Mar: 9:30am–4pm Thu–Mon ⬛ nts.org.uk 🔗

Said to be one of the most beguiling gardens in Scotland, Crarae is considered of international importance and is a member of "Glorious Gardens of Argyll and Bute" (*gardens-of-argyll.co.uk*).

**Weapons in the Armoury Hall, Inveraray Castle**

The gardens now resemble a Himalayan ravine, nourished by the warmth of the Gulf Stream and the region's high rainfall. The outstanding and rare collection of Himalayan rhododendrons flourishes here, and is at its best in spring. The gardens are also home to plants from Tasmania, New Zealand and the US.

# 10 Arduaine Gardens
📍 F3 🏠 Nr Oban 🕐 Mar–Oct: 10am–5pm daily 🌐 nts.org.uk 🔗

A dazzling assembly of rhododendrons, azaleas, magnolias and hosts of global species from the Pacific Islands to the Himalayas. Arduaine (p53) is beautifully situated on a promontory between sea lochs, and glories in the warm winds from the Gulf Stream.

## THE WONDERFUL WORLD OF CRARAE GARDENS

Lady Grace Campbell began to lay out the gardens in 1912, making exciting use of plant specimens that her nephew Reginald Farrer brought back from his travels to the Himalayas.

On the higher ground is the forest-garden, a feature that is found nowhere else in Britain, where more than 100 tree species grow under forest conditions on their own plots.

## A DAY IN THE TROSSACHS

### Morning

Reserve your morning cruise aboard the *Rob Roy III* or *Lady of the Lake* (lochkatrine.com).

Leaving **Glasgow** by 8:15am, drive north on the A81 to **Strathblane** and **Aberfoyle**. You are now in the scenic **Trossachs** *(p107)*. Park at the **Trossachs Pier** for a 10:30am cruise on **Loch Katrine** *(p50)*, a gorgeous loch.

Arriving back at 12:30pm, a short drive takes you to Kilmahog (great name, and the Woollen Mill is worth a visit if you're curious about knitwear). Head on to Callander, where you can stop for lunch at one of several restaurants, or buy delicious pies at the **Mhor Bread & Tearoom** *(mhorbread.net)* and picnic by the river.

### Afternoon

Carry on to **Doune**, **Dunblane** and **Bridge of Allan**. There are many temptations en route, including the **Doune Castle** *(p110)*, a cathedral and a motor museum.

If not, head to **Wallace Monument** *(p107)* before 4pm, and earlier than that in winter. Enjoy the history and the panoramic views of the area, including the craggy heights of **Stirling Castle** *(p107)*.

Head back to Glasgow for an early dinner in the city centre *(p105)*. For those who can wait, Edinburgh or St Andrews *(p96)* are only slightly further towards the east (each about an hour's drive).

# The Best of the Rest

### 1. Doune Castle
**F4** **Doune** **Apr–Sep: 9:30am–5:30pm daily; Oct–Mar: 10am–4pm daily** **historicenvironment.scot**
The highlight of this 14th-century castle is the majestic Lord's Hall, with its musicians' gallery and double fireplace.

### 2. Bonawe Historic Iron Furnace
**E3** **Taynuilt** **Apr–Sep: 9:30am–5:30pm daily** **historicenvironment.scot**
These superbly preserved charcoal-fuelled ironworks, set by Loch Etive, were last operational in 1876.

### 3. St Conan's Kirk
**E3** **Lochawe village** **Apr–Sep: 8am–6pm daily; Oct–Mar: 9am–5pm daily** **stconanskirk.org.uk**
With an eclectic architectural style, this remarkable church has three chapels, one of which contains a marble effigy of Robert the Bruce.

### 4. Cruachan Hollow Mountain Power Station
**E3** **Nr Lochawe** **Hours vary, check website** **visitcruachan.co.uk**
Tunnels and underground caverns make this massive hydroelectric plant seem like a science-fiction set.

### 5. Oban
**E3** **oban.org.uk**
This busy harbour town is best seen from McCaig's Folly. There are many local attractions here and ferries travelling to Mull, Coll, Colonsay, Tiree and the Western Isles.

### 6. Crinan Canal
**F3** **scottishcanal.co.uk**
Take a stroll along this scenic 16-km (9-mile) canal, completed in 1801. It has a total of 15 locks, and is now used by yachts and fishing boats. The best places to see them are at Ardrishaig, Cairnbaan or Crinan.

Intricately designed tombstone, Kilmartin Church

### 7. Auchindrain Township
**F3** **Nr Inveraray** **Hours vary, check website** **auchindrain.org.uk**
A novel outdoor museum of restored thatched cottages, Auchindrain displays the past styles of West Highland life.

### 8. Scottish Crannog Centre
**E4** **Kenmore** **Apr–Oct: 10am–5:30pm daily** **crannog.co.uk**
The little-known and ancient art of building *crannogs* (defensive home-steads built on stilts in lochs) is brought to life at the museum here.

### 9. Kintyre
**G3** **wildaboutargyll.co.uk**
Paul McCartney sang about this glorious peninsula, which has miles of beaches, a top golf course (Machrihanish) and the ethereal cave crucifixion painting on Davaar Island.

### 10. Kilmartin Glen
**F3** **historicenvironment.scot**
Inhabited for 5,000 years, the area is dense with archaeological remains such as standing stones and temples. Pause at Kilmartin Church for their collection of early Christian crosses.

# Places to Eat and Drink

### 1. The Roman Camp
**F4** **Callander** **romancamp hotel.co.uk · £££**

Fancy curtains, deep sofas and blazing fires make this hotel a delight, and the restaurant excels. The Sunday lunch special, rump of lamb, is a winner.

### 2. Marina Restaurant
**F3** **Portavadie, Loch Fyne** **portavadie.com · ££**

Loch Fyne oysters and fresh seafood are served in this lovely restaurant that offers splendid views of Kintyre and the distant Arran Hills.

### 3. Ee-Usk
**E3** **North Pier, Oban** **eeusk. com · ££**

Fresh seafood straight from Oban harbour is served in a modern building with huge windows and sea views.

### 4. Loch Fyne Oyster Bar
**F3** **Cairndow, nr Inveraray** **lochfyne.com · ££**

This brilliant oyster bar offers an ocean of seafood, including loin of cod, haddock, lobster and, of course, oysters.

### 5. The Drover's Inn
**F4** **Inverarnan, Loch Lomond** **droversinn.co.uk · ££**

A flagstone floor, cobwebbed walls and a menagerie of stuffed animals to fight your way past – it's quite an experience. Good ol' pub grub and amber fluid flow all day.

**Dish of crab claws at the Loch Fyne Oyster Bar**

---

**PRICE CATEGORIES**

For a three-course meal for one with half a bottle of wine (or equivalent meal), taxes and extra charges.

**£ under £30  ££ £30–60  £££ over £60**

---

### 6. The Kailyard
**F4** **Perth Rd, Dunblane FK15 OHG** **doubletreedunblane.com · ££**

Fine Scottish produce is served at this hotel restaurant, run by celebrity chef Nick Nairn. The dishes served include Scotch beef and Scrabster sole. It also has a good vegetarian menu.

### 7. Starfish
**F2** **Castle St, Tarbert** **starfishoftarbert.com · ££**

Set in a picturesque fishing village, this friendly and relaxed restaurant with local art on the walls serves up langoustines, lobster, scallops, crab and other seafood – all of which is landed daily at the nearby quay.

### 8. The Waterfront
**E4** **Kenmore** **henmoreclub.com · ££**

Overlooking Loch Tay, this sleek and modern restaurant serves dishes prepared with fresh local produce. Try the haddock, venison and sea trout. Vegetarian options are available.

### 9. Tigh-an-Truish
**F3** **Clachan, Isle of Seil** **tighantruish.co.uk · ££**

Old-world inn by the famous "Bridge over the Atlantic"; you half expect pirates to breeze in. Real ale and delicious local food.

### 10. Hermann's
**F4** **58 Broad St, Stirling** **hermanns.co.uk · ££**

A long-standing local favourite, famed for fine Scottish steaks and Austrian dishes such as schnitzel and *spätzle*.

# GRAMPIAN AND MORAY

Covering ice-sculpted mountains, craggy coastline and swathes of quilted farmland, the northeastern corner of Scotland is home to a veritable medley of landscapes. On its western edge lies the Cairngorms, a loch-dotted granite massif that lures walkers, cyclists and skiers with the promise of adventure, while in the centre sits Balmoral, a grand holiday home for royalty surrounded by rolling hills and forest. The region's coastline is lined with a mixture of pretty beaches, dramatic cliffs and enchanting fishing villages, while dotted across its landscape are countless castles, including Fyvie and Cawdor. Winding though it all is the sparkling River Spey, the country's heartland of whisky production.

## 1 Dunnottar Castle

 E6  Nr Stonehaven  Hours vary, chech website (may be closed during bad weather)  dunnottarcastle.co.uk 

Standing strikingly on a rock, few castles match Dunnottar's setting or have endured such intense bombardments. In 1651, while harbouring the Scottish royalty who were secretly smuggled out by a brave woman, it withstood an eight-month siege by the English. Some 800 years of attack have taken their toll, but Dunnottar remains a mythical sight. It featured in *Victor Frankenstein*, the 2015 sci-fi film adaptation of Mary Shelley's 1818 novel, starring Daniel Radcliffe, and also featured as Elsinore in Franco Zeffirelli's *Hamlet*.

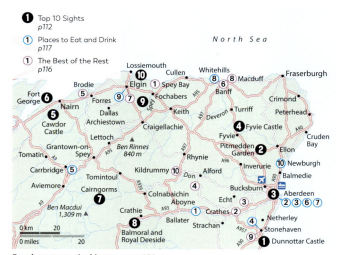

- **1** Top 10 Sights *p112*
- **1** Places to Eat and Drink *p117*
- **1** The Best of the Rest *p116*

*For places to stay in this area, see p151*

**Beautifully landscaped Great Garden, Pitmedden Garden**

## 2 Pitmedden Garden

🅟 D6 🏠 Ellon ⏰ Grounds: dawn–dusk daily; Garden & museum: Apr–late Sep: 10:30am–4:30pm daily 🆆 nts.org.uk 🗲

The striking symmetry of the formal Great Garden is unique. The wildlife gardens and the Museum of Farming Life are hits, too.

## 3 Aberdeen

🅟 D6 🏠 Grampian 🆆 visit abdn.com

The "Granite City" has beautiful buildings, year-round floral displays and a beach fringed with entertainment, including the Beach Leisure Centre and the Aberdeen Science Centre (*aberdeensciencecentre.org*), a science discovery complex. Provost Skene's House (once home to a

17th-century *provost*, or mayor, of Aberdeen) is the oldest building (*aagm.co.uk*), dating from 1545, while Marischal College (*abdn.ac.uk*) is one of the world's largest granite edifices. The Maritime Museum (*aberdeencity. gov.uk*) charts the nautical world from shipbuilding to shipwrecks, while the Art Gallery (*aberdeencity.gov.uk*) combines temporary contemporary shows with a permanent collection spanning the 19th–20th centuries.

## 4 Fyvie Castle

🅟 D6 🏠 Nr Turriff ⏰ Castle: Apr–Dec: 10:30am–4:30pm Thu–Sun; Garden: 9am–sunset daily 🆆 nts.org.uk 🗲🗲

Dating from 1390, this formidable building, which once hosted Charles I, is one of the finest examples of Scottish Baronial architecture. Its life through the ages is testified to by the mix of contemporary panelling, 17th-century plasterwork and treasure trove of collectable paintings, arms and armour. The restored 19th-century Victorian walled garden specializes in Scottish fruit and vegetables. The castle has guided tours only.

**Bishop Elphinstone's tomb at Old Aberdeen**

**Fine portraits and furniture at Cawdor Castle**

# 5 Cawdor Castle

🔲 D4 🏠 Nr Nairn 🕐 May–early Oct: 10am–5pm daily 🌐 cawdorcastle.com ↗

A private home, handed down through the generations since the time when Macbeth lived here (or so legend has it). Cawdor Castle is full of history and delight, with creepy relics, magnificent trees and a garden maze.

# 6 Fort George

🔲 D4 🏠 Inverness 🌐 historicenvironment.scot

On a peninsula jutting into the Moray Firth is this vast fort complex, built 250 years ago and still used as army barracks today. Impressive defences now guard a vintage armoury. Check out the special summer events.

# 7 Cairngorms

A superb range of mountain peaks *(p42)* surrounded by pine forests and lochs. Ideal for testing walks, lively watersports and inspiring scenery.

# 8 Balmoral and Royal Deeside

🔲 D5 🏠 Balmoral Estate, Ballater 🕐 Apr–Jul: 10am–5pm daily; Oct–Dec: hours vary, chech website 🌐 balmoralcastle.com ↗

Queen Victoria bought this castle in 1852. Balmoral, bordering the salmon pools of the River Dee, remains the holiday home of the monarch to this day and, consequently, the rolling countryside around the banks of the river has taken on the royal moniker. The royal family traditionally spend every August at Balmoral, hence the estate is off-limits to visitors during this time. Cast an eye round the castle's sumptuous ballroom, then make the most of the enchanting forest walks.

# 9 The Whisky Trail

Seven of Scotland's finest malt whisky distilleries *(p70)* invite you inside. Apart from the magic of the shining copper stills, the once-secretive process of whisky-making is revealed, enthusiasm infused and the precious *uisge beatha* (water of life) consumed.

# 10 Moray Coast Villages

🔲 C5–6

These charming communities thrived in the herring boom of the 19th century, but today only Lossiemouth, Buckie (with its excellent Drifter

**Charming village of Crovie on the Moray Coast**

Museum), Macduff and Fraserburgh continue as fishing ports. For many visitors, Crovie (pronounced "crivie") is the pick of the bunch. Access from the car park is by foot only, its picturesque street strung out below the cliffs – it truly is a fabulous setting. The walk to Gardenstown is an adventure for the sure-footed. Findhorn – famous for its spiritual community – is beautifully located on a sandy lagoon. A self-drive tour of the coastal road (highly recommended) will reveal a dozen other villages, each one possessing its own unique character.

### VICTORIA AND ALBERT'S BALMORAL

It was the riverside setting that Victoria fell for in 1848 when she first visited Balmoral. And it was her husband Albert who worked with the Aberdeen-born architect William Smith to create the white granite palace that replaced the old castle and stands here still, a medley of fantastical turrets typical of the Baronial style.

**Magnificent wilderness of the Cairngorms National Park**

## A DAY'S DRIVING TOUR

### Morning

Leave **Aberdeen** (p113) around 9am and drive on the A93 through Deeside's splendid scenery to Crathie, where you'll find the castle in **Balmoral** opening its gates. If, however, you're outside Balmoral's opening season, then visit **Crathes Castle** or **Drum Castle** (p116).

Return to **Ballater**, the nearest town to Balmoral Castle which you passed through on the way, but this time take the B976 on the south of the river. There are plenty of places to eat.

### Afternoon

While browsing the shops in Ballater, look out for royal insignias: they indicate Elizabeth II's favourite establishments.

From Ballater find the A939 and drive north on this twisting road. The terrain is wild, heathery moorland and mountainous. The road takes you past **Corgarff Castle**, and on to **Tomintoul**, one of the highest villages in Scotland. From here, take the B9008 to the distillery of **Glenlivet** (p70) for a tour of their whisky-making vats, stills and barrels, and a tasting. Tours last about 75 minutes; the tastings, unfortunately, much less.

Spend the night around **Dufftown** or **Keith** and plan to drive to **Portsoy** on the coast road either east or west the next day. The tour is about 150 km (90 miles) in total.

# The Best of the Rest

### 1. Moray Firth
🛈 D4 🏛 Moray 🌐 morayspeyside.com
Renowned for its wildlife-spotting opportunities, most notably from the Chanonry viewing point, Moray Firth is home to a wealth of marine life. Harbour seals, bottlenose dolphins and several species of whale come here to feed. Dolphin spotting tours are available, and you can learn more about Moray Firth's sealife at the WDC Scottish Dolphin Centre *(dolphincentre.whales.org)*.

### 2. Crathes Castle
🛈 D6 🏛 Banchory ⏰ Hours vary, check website 🌐 nts.org.uk 🚻
A 16th-century tower house, with a traditional Great Hall. There are topiary and plant sales Easter to October.

### 3. Drum Castle
🛈 D6 🏛 Nr Banchory ⏰ Hours vary, check website 🌐 nts.org.uk 🚻
This is one of the three oldest surviving tower houses in Scotland.

### 4. Craigievar Castle
🛈 D6 ⏰ Hours vary, check website 🌐 nts.org.uk 🚻
A distinctive shade of pastel pink, this charming castle is said to have been the inspiration behind Walt Disney's Cinderella Castle.

### 5. Brodie Castle
🛈 D4 🏛 Forres, nr Nairn ⏰ Hours vary, check website 🌐 nts.org.uk 🚻
This turreted castle has a magnificent collection of furniture, ceramics and artwork, including works by 17th-century Dutch masters.

### 6. Duff House Gallery
🛈 C6 🏛 Banff Tel ⏰ Apr–Sep: 9:30am–1pm & 2–5pm Thu–Sun; Oct–Mar: 10am–4pm Fri–Sun 🌐 historic environment.scot 🚻
The collection at this Georgian mansion includes works by Ramsay and Raeburn, as well as El Greco.

**Bottlenose dolphins playing in the Moray Firth**

### 7. Elgin Cathedral
🛈 C5 🏛 Moray ⏰ Apr–Sep: 9:30am–5:30pm daily; Oct–Mar: 10am–4pm daily 🌐 historicenvironment.scot 🚻
Burned out of spite by the Wolf of Badenoch in 1390, this cathedral's picturesque ruins draw a crowd.

### 8. Macduff Marine Aquarium
🛈 C5 🏛 11 High Shore, Macduff ⏰ Apr–Oct: 10am–5pm Mon–Fri, 11am–5pm Sat & Sun; Nov–Mar: 11am–4pm Sat–Wed 🌐 macduff-aquarium.org.uk 🚻
With a vast central tank recreating the submarine world of kelp reefs, this museum reveals the sealife of Scottish waters. Marine life here includes sharks, rays, octopus and seahorses.

### 9. Stonehaven
🛈 E6 🏛 Aberdeenshire 🌐 stonehaven openairpool.co.uk
Close to Dunnottar Castle *(p112)*, this seaside resort has a heated open-air Olympic-size swimming pool.

### 10. Kildrummy Castle
🛈 D5 🏛 Nr Alford ⏰ Apr–Sep: 9:30am–5:30pm Sun–Mon 🌐 historic environment.scot 🚻
The once "noblest of northern castles" is now a grandiose ruin but retains many unique 13th-century features.

# Places to Eat and Drink

**PRICE CATEGORIES**

For a three-course meal for one with half a bottle of wine (or equivalent meal), taxes and extra charges.

**£** under £30 **££** £30–60 **£££** over £60

## 1. At the Sign of the Black Faced Sheep
**ⓜ** D5 **ⓐ** Ballater Rd, Aboyne **Ⓦ** black facedsheep.co.uk · **£**
Emporium with an upmarket coffee shop serving interesting sandwiches, sun-dried tomato scones, seafood platters, daily specials and great cakes.

## 2. The Spiritualist Aberdeen
**ⓜ** D6 **ⓐ** 67 Langstane Pl, Aberdeen **Ⓦ** thespiritualistaberdeen.co.uk · **£**
This trendy bar-restaurant has an extensive cocktail list and serves an assortment of fusion-cuisine bar meals, snacks and nibbles.

## 3. 210 Bistro
**ⓜ** D6 **ⓐ** 210 South Market St, Aberdeen **Ⓒ** Sun **Ⓦ** 210bistro.com · **££**
The downstairs café and bar forms a relaxing anteroom between bustling Market Street and the upstairs restaurant with its minimalist decor and harbour views. The menu features fresh and beautifully presented Scottish dishes.

## 4. Tolbooth Restaurant
**ⓜ** E6 **ⓐ** Stonehaven **Ⓦ** thetolbooth restaurant.co.uk · **££**
With fabulous harbour views, this little restaurant in Stonehaven's oldest building is a great spot to treat yourself to inventive seafood dishes such as curry dusted monkfish.

## 5. Anderson's
**ⓜ** D4 **ⓐ** Boat of Garten **Ⓦ** andersons restaurant.co.uk · **££**
Classy little restaurant offering a short, excellent menu that combines Scottish and European cuisines beautifully.

## 6. The Silver Darling
**ⓜ** D6 **ⓐ** Pocra Quay, Aberdeen **Ⓦ** thesilverdarling.co.uk · **££**
One of the best restaurants in the country, this seafood emporium overlooks the Aberdeen harbour.

## 7. Moonfish Café
**ⓜ** D6 **ⓐ** 9 Correction Wynd, Aberdeen **Ⓦ** moonfishcafe.co.uk · **££**
Tucked away in a lane, this place is known for some of Aberdeen's most inventive fare.

## 8. The Seafield Arms
**ⓜ** D5–6 **ⓐ** 5 Chapel St, Whitehills, nr Banff **Ⓦ** seafieldarmscullen.co.uk · **££**
Set on the Moray Firth, this inn focuses on seafood dishes. Try the baked haddock with tiger prawns.

## 9. The Sunninghill Hotel
**ⓜ** C5 **ⓐ** Hay St, Elgin **Ⓦ** sunninghill hotel.com · **££**
Popular with locals, this hotel serves traditional Scottish dishes such as steak pie and fresh haddock with chips.

## 10. Cock and Bull
**ⓜ** D6 **ⓐ** Ellon Rd, Balmedie **Ⓦ** thecock andbull.co.uk · **££**
Rustic meets trendy in this blend of country inn and contemporary gastro-pub. Try the fish cakes or a juicy burger.

**Cosy interior, At the Sign of the Black Faced Sheep**

# THE HIGHLANDS

Epitomizing Scotland for many, this vast and sparsely populated region is known for its stunning scenery. To the west lie the craggy mountain ranges of Assynt, Torridon and Glencoe – the last of which sits close to Ben Nevis, Britain's tallest peak – while to the east is Glen Affric, a rugged valley covered in heather and Caledonian pines. Sprinkled across the Highlands are countless lochs, including inky blue Loch Ness, as well as an impressive collection of castles, among them the iconic Eilean Donan. While most settlements tend to be small here, places like Inverness, the Highland capital, and Fort William are home to plenty of places to eat and drink, and make excellent starting points for exploring the region.

| | |
|---|---|
| **1** | Top 10 Sights *p119* |
| **①** | Places to Eat and Drink *p123* |
| **①** | The Best of the Rest *p122* |

*For places to stay in this area, see p151*

# 1 Culloden Battlefield

**D4** nts.org.uk

The last battle on British soil, 16th April 1746, was a defeat for Bonnie Prince Charlie and the Jacobites *(p10)*. The slaughter by the "Bloody Butcher's" (the Duke of Cumberland's) Hanoverian army was quick and brutal. The desolate battlefield is gradually being restored to its appearance at the time of the bloodshed. Visitors can roam the battlefield, visit the clan graves and experience the audio-visual displays at the NTS Visitor Centre. The Memorial Cairn, which was erected here in 1881, stands 6 m (20 ft) high. The story is well illustrated in the visitor centre.

# 2 Loch Ness

Centuries ago, the Great Glen was born of a geological rift that split Scotland from coast to coast. Glaciers deepened the trench resulting in a long valley of mountains and deep lochs. Loch Ness *(p36)* is its main attraction and the country's largest body of water, with arresting views, the mystery of its reclusive monster and the evocative ruins of Urquhart Castle.

Inverness Castle on the banks of the River Ness

# 3 Inverness

**D4** visitinvernessloch ness.com

A fast-growing city with a small-town feel, Inverness is home to a majestic red sandstone castle *(invernesscastle.scot)*. Visit the Inverness Museum and Art Gallery *(highlifehighland.com)*, which provides an interesting insight into Highland heritage, as well as excellent temporary exhibitions. There's also the 1593 Abertarff House *(nts.org.uk)*, the oldest house in Inverness, and the sublimely peaceful Ness Islands Walk.

# 4 Ben Nevis and Fort William

**E3** bennevis.co.uk

Standing at a whopping 1,345 m (4,413 ft), Britain's highest peak, Ben Nevis *(p55)*, offers walking routes to suit all abilities. The views from the summit are breathtaking and well worth the effort to get there. Note that the peak is frequently shrouded in mist, so some may prefer the drive to Glen Nevis, a more reliable alternative. Fort William *(p36)*, one of the major towns on the west coast, lies below the mountain, with plenty of attractions. Its West Highland Museum *(westhigh landmuseum.org.uk)* has many Jacobite relics, and *Treasures of the Earth* exhibits glittering heaps of gems.

Ruins of Urquhart Castle along the Loch Ness shore

### 5 Glenfinnan Monument and Jacobite Steam Train

🅿 E3  🆆 nts.org.uk; westcoast railways.co.uk

This is another memorial to the Jacobite uprising led by Bonnie Prince Charlie, on the site where his campaign began. Here, a visitor centre explains the history. Take time to marvel at the nearby viaduct, which will be especially familiar to fans of *Harry Potter*, as the Hogwarts Express puffed along it in several of the films. The Jacobite Steam Train, which doubles as the Hogwarts Express, runs the scenic route from Fort William to Mallaig.

### 6 Eilean Donan Castle

🅿 D3  🅰 Off A87, near Dornie  🕐 Feb–Dec: 10am–4pm daily (Apr–Sep: to 6pm)  🆆 eilean donancastle.com 🔗

Restored in the 13th century, this majestic fortress of Clan Macrae stands on a picturesque island on the road to Skye. The rooms hold numerous exhibits such as a lock of Bonnie Prince Charlie's hair. The castle has also been used as a film set, featuring in both *Highlander* and the James Bond epic *The World Is Not Enough*.

### 7 Attadale Gardens

🅿 D3  🅰 Attadale, nr. Kyle of Lochalsh  🕐 Mar–Oct: 10am–5pm daily  🆆 attadalegardens.com

The lushly landscaped estate of an 18th-century manor house, Attadale Gardens is a peaceful spot. Highlights include ancient paths winding through woodland and rhododendrons, a Japanese garden and a sculpture trail.

### 8 Torridon

🅿 D3  🆆 nts.org.uk

Flanked by a long sea loch, the red sandstone buttresses of Beinn Alligin, Ben Dearg, Liathach *(p54)* and Beinn Eighe create an arresting image. The Torridon Estate has some of the oldest mountains on earth, and is home to red deer, wildcats and wild goats. Peregrine falcons and golden eagles nest in the sandstone mass of Beinn Eighe, above Torridon village, with views over Applecross towards Skye. From Little Diabaig you can walk a delightful coastal path to Alligin Shuas, or to Craig. The National Trust for Scotland runs an informative Countryside Centre.

---

#### RETURN OF THE BONNIE PRINCE

Set on reclaiming the British Crown for the Stuart line, Bonnie Prince Charlie landed on the west coast of Scotland in 1745 with but a handful of men. His temerity, as well as widespread support for the Jacobite cause, won over many Scots, and when he came to raise his standard at Glenfinnan, numbers swelled as clans such as the Camerons rallied to his side.

Jacobite Steam Train chugging
along the Glenfinnan Viaduct

# 9 Inverewe Gardens

📍 C3 🏠 Nr Poolewe ⏰ Jan–late
May & Sep: 9:45am–4pm daily
(Jun–Aug: to 5pm) 🌐 nts.org.uk ↗

The sheer richness and variety of
plant life growing here *(p52)* in
what many consider to be a cold
wilderness is a tribute to a plant
enthusiast's vision and hard work,
nature's bounty and the surprising
benign effects of warm Atlantic
winds. Now one of Scotland's leading botanical gardens, Inverewe has
Blue Nile lilies, rhododendrons from
China and the tallest Australian gum
trees in Britain.

# 10 Glencoe

📍 E3 🌐 nts.org.uk

A rugged mountain range gathered
into gorgeous scenery through which
the twisting main road seems to
creep submissively. A favourite skiing,
mountaineering and walking area,
and infamous for the terrible 1692
massacre of Clan MacDonald.

**Dramatic landscape of Glencoe
in the Highlands**

## A HIGHLAND DAY TRIP

### Morning

Pack a picnic in **Inverness** *(p119)*.
There are lots of picnicking
possibilities on this route, so make
sure to take one.

Leave Inverness by 10am, taking
the B852 to **Dores** and driving
along the south side of **Loch Ness**
*(p36)*. Try to stop off at the **Falls
of Foyers** *(p65)*.

Enjoy the hill-country drive to
**Fort Augustus** *(p37)*, and pop
in for a coffee at **The Lock
Inn** *(the-lockinn.co.uk)*, right
beside the canal.

Drive along the A82 on the
north side of Loch Ness (stop at
**Invermoriston** to view the river
pools and old bridge) and visit
**Urquhart Castle** *(p36)*. This is a
great spot to enjoy that picnic.

### Afternoon

Having recharged your batteries
sufficiently, visit one of the **Loch
Ness Monster Visitor Centres**
*(p37)* in Drumnadrochit.

Refill your thermos in
Drumnadrochit, then take the
A831 to Cannich, and the minor
road to **Glen Affric** *(p112)*.

Enjoy an hour's walk in this
renowned beauty spot, before
returning to the bustle of
Inverness via **Kilmorack** and
the south shore of the **Beauly
Firth**. The entire round trip is
about 185 km (115 miles).

# The Best of the Rest

### 1. Plockton
🅿 D3
Prime candidate for the title of Scotland's prettiest west coast village, Plockton has sea, palm trees and a Rare Breeds Farm.

### 2. Glen Affric
🅿 D3
Accessed from the east at Cannich, this glen is an example of nature's outstanding beauty. At the western end, near Morvich, there's a walk to the breathtaking Falls of Glomach.

### 3. Gairloch Heritage Museum
🅿 C3 🏛 Gairloch 🕐 10am–4:30pm Mon–Sat 🌐 gairlochmuseum.org 🔗
Housed within an old nuclear bunker, this museum has displays on the local land and people; the star exhibit being the Poolewe Hoard, a stash of Bronze Age artifacts discovered in 1877. Look out, too, for the "midgeater", an ingenious contraption designed to repel midges.

### 4. Dunrobin Castle
🅿 C4 🏛 Golspie 🕐 Hours vary, check website 🌐 dunrobincastle.co.uk 🔗
A stately home befitting its wealthy landowners, the dukes of Sutherland. The castle has towers, turrets and a palatial interior. There are also garden falconry displays here.

### 5. The Hydroponicum, Achiltibuie
🅿 C3 🌐 thehydroponicum.com 🔗
The glasshouse here is known for cultivating various plants. It is advisable to book ahead before your visit.

### 6. Ullapool
🅿 C3
Delightful grid-plan village with Gaelic street names, boat trips, ferries to the Western Isles, a museum and the dream-world Assynt Mountains. Visit Corrieshalloch Gorge en route.

### 7. The Road to Applecross
🅿 D2
To get to this small coastal village, you'll have to drive up the road climbing 750 m (2,000 ft) in steep zigzags to the Bealach na Bà (Pass of the Cattle). The scenery – with views across to Isle of Skye – is magnificent, and from here the gradual descent into Applecross begins.

### 8. Timespan
🅿 C5 🏛 Helmsdale 🕐 Mar–Oct: 10am–5pm daily 🌐 timespan.org.uk 🔗
This heritage centre is well worth a visit to understand the effect of the 19th-century Clearances, which is even visible today.

### 9. Dornoch Cathedral
🅿 C4 🌐 dornoch-cathedral.com
Madonna chose it for her wedding and 16 earls of Sutherland requested it for their burials; Dornoch is an impressive 13th-century cathedral.

### 10. Loch Morar
🅿 E3 🌐 lochmorar.org.uk
This enormous loch is 18 km (12 miles) long and offers great fishing, walking and wildlife watching – otters, sea eagles and golden eagles, and (reputedly) its own monster, Morag.

**Red-roofed cottage en route to Applecross**

# Places to Eat and Drink

**Well-stocked bar at the Clachaig Inn**

## 1. Uile-bheist Distillery

📍 D4 📍 Ness Bank, Inverness
🕐 10am–7pm daily 🌐 uilebheist. com · £££

Launched in 2023, Uile-bheist uses technology to minimize its carbon impact while producing single malt whiskies and artisan ales using locally sourced barley and yeasts.

## 2. Old Pines

📍 E3 📍 Spean Bridge 🌐 oldpines. co.uk · ££

Conscientiously organic, devoted to sourcing local ingredients and a member of the "slow food" movement, this little restaurant has earned a big name.

## 3. Airds Hotel

📍 E3 📍 Port Appin, Appin
🌐 airds-hotel.com · £££

A country hotel restaurant with crisp, white table linen and candlelight, and a reputation for serving the best of Scottish produce.

## 4. The Mustard Seed

📍 D4 📍 16 Fraser St, Inverness
🌐 mustardseedrestaurant.co.uk · ££

With its stylish interior and riverside location, the Mustard Seed produces some of the finest modern Scottish cuisine in the Highlands.

## 5. Applecross Inn

📍 D2 📍 Applecross, Wester Ross
🌐 applecrossinn.co.uk · ££

Spectacularly located beyond Britain's highest mountain pass, this pub overlooks the Isle of Skye. Local seafood is served, and there is also live music some evenings.

## 6. Summer Isles Hotel

📍 C3 📍 Achiltibuie, Ross-shire
🌐 summerisleshotel.com · ££

This pet-friendly restaurant serves more formal meals. Sample dishes such as monkfish tail with bacon, or baked halibut with parmesan crumb.

## 7. The Ceilidh Place

📍 C3 📍 14 West Argyle St, Ullapool
🌐 theceilidhplace.com · ££

A hotel-restaurant-bar *(p150)* and a vibrant entertainment venue. You can get everything from a snack to a feast here, plus live music and dance.

## 8. Clachaig Inn

📍 E3 📍 Glencoe 🌐 clachaig.com · ££

A legendary haunt of walkers, this hotel offers a wide range of food and is known for its bar. Clachaig Inn is as essential to Highland trekkers as a first Munro.

## 9. Plockton Shores

📍 D3 📍 30 Harbour St, Plockton
🌐 plocktonshores.com · ££

The fruits of the west coast are served up with love and aplomb, on the shores of beautiful Loch Carron.

## 10. Crannog at Garisson West

📍 E3 📍 4 Cameron Sq, Fort William
🌐 garrisonwest.co.uk · ££

Fresh seafood complemented by generous helpings. The atmosphere is welcoming, with efficient service. Reservations are essential.

Epic scenery along the zigzagging Bealach na Bà

# WEST COAST ISLANDS

**More than 600 islands lie scattered along Scotland's Atlantic coastline, from seabird-clustered islets to bigger islands sprinkled with towns and villages. Found to the north, Lewis and Harris is the largest island, with the famed Isle of Skye following closely behind. Further south lie the Small Isles, while beyond these are the likes of Mull and the whisky-producing isles of Jura and Islay.**

Top 10 Sights
*p126*

Places to Eat and Drink
*p131*

The Best of the Rest
*p130*

*For places to stay in this area, see p151*

## 1 Islay
F2–G2

The most southerly of Scotland's Western Isles, Islay is a thriving island, with nine distilleries producing peaty Highland malts. Bowmore, the island's capital, is known for its unusual grid layout and Round Church. It is home to a great distillery. Britain's most impressive 8th-century Celtic cross can be found at Kildalton. Some of Islay's superb beaches support a variety of birdlife and more than 250 species of birds have been spotted here.

## 2 Jura
F2

The wildest and least visited of all the Hebridean islands. Overrun by red deer and dominated by its central hills, the Paps, Jura has been little affected by modernity: a single road links the ferry port to the main settlement, Craighouse. If you revel in solitude and rugged scenery, the walks are tremendous.

**The famous Red deer on the Isle of Jura**

## 3 Iona and Staffa
**☑ F2–E2**

A sparkling island of white-sand beaches, Iona has an active crofting community. Many visitors come daily in summer to visit the famous restored abbey where St Columba came in 563 to establish a missionary centre; 48 Scottish kings are said to be buried here. Staffa contains Scotland's greatest natural wonder: Fingal's Cave, formed by thousands of basalt columns, which inspired German composer Felix Mendelssohn to pen his famous *Hebrides Overture*.

## 4 Mull
**☑ E2–F2**

The largest of the Inner Hebridean Islands, Mull features rough moorlands, the rocky peak of Ben More and a splendid beach at Calgary. Most roads follow the coastline, affording wonderful sea views. On a promontory east of Craignure lies the 13th-century Duart Castle, home of the chief of Clan Maclean. Tobermory, at the northern end of the Mull, is the place to unwind. Its colourful seafront is a classic postcard scene. Built as a fishing village in 1788, it is now a popular port for yachts.

**Strolling on a white-sand beach, Iona**

## 5 Colonsay and Oronsay
**☑ F2**

Colonsay has provided farmland and shelter to people since at least the Bronze Age, and many of their tombs and standing stones remain. Old traditions persist here, and Colonsay is still a strong crofting *(p128)* and fishing community. Wild flowers and birds thrive on this terrain, but it is the coastline that lures most visitors. Check the tides and walk out to the adjacent little island of Oronsay, with its ruined priory.

**Carved Celtic cross at the Oronsay Priory**

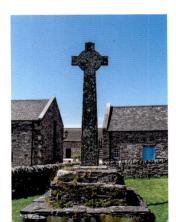

## 6 Coll
☑ E2

Wild flowers, migrant birds, otters, standing stones, active crofts, a castle and a surfeit of beaches make this a particularly varied and delightful island.

## 7 Small Isles
☑ D2–E2

While Canna and Muck are home to traditional farming communities,

**The Callanish Stones on the Isle of Lewis**

Rum was once the private playground of a rich industrialist; you can see his incredible fantasy home, Kinloch Castle, as well as wander the island's towering mountains. Eigg was a landmark community buyout, and the islander-owners now run a crafts shop and tours. Their ceilidhs *(p49)* are legendary. The Sgurr of Eigg, a sugarloaf spur, yields fabulous views.

## 8 Isle of Lewis
☑ C2

Lewis is the largest and most populous of the Western Isles. Although geographically one island, the northern half is called Lewis and, the southern half, Harris. Together, they are world-famous for producing tweed. One thing you absolutely must see is the spectacular 4,500-year-old stone circle known as the Callanais (Calanais) Stones, which resonates with a deep sense of mystery. Arnol has an engaging traditional "blackhouse" (blackened by smoke) and Carloway, the ruined walls of a remarkable Iron Age broch. Harris is more mountainous. Driving the "Golden Road" reveals the best scenery; stop at the stunning Luskentyre beach, with its miles of white sands and blue-green water.

**White sands of the Cockle Strand on Barra**

## 9 Barra
### ⚐ D1
This small isle encapsulates all the charm of the Hebrides: scintillating beaches, the culture of the Gaels, tranquillity and road-priority to sheep. No matter how you arrive, it will make a deep impression: planes land on the sands of Cockle Beach, while ferries sail into a delightful bay where the 11th-century Kisimul Castle poses on an island of its own. A soothing place to unwind.

## 10 Isle of Skye
Mountainous, misty and magical, Skye (p34) is an island of dramatic scenery, with an ancient castle, an idolized distillery and plenty more attractions.

## TWO DAYS AROUND MULL

### Morning
Leave **Oban** (p110) on a mid-morning ferry for the 45-minute trip across to the **Isle of Mull** (p127). Book your tickets ahead of time (calmac.co.uk).

You might want to spend the day on a wildlife tour, as the island is home to sea eagles, otters and red deer. Wildlife and sealife boat trips with Staffa Tours (staffatours.com), depart from Tobermory. Otherwise head for **Duart Castle**, the 13th-century home of the Macleans. After exploring the castle and gardens, have lunch in the delightfully quaint tearoom.

### Afternoon
There are plenty of options for walks on Mull or you can drive to **Calgary Bay** to see the stunning white shell beach. Alternatively, make for **Tobermory**, the picture-postcard fishing port that is the island's main town.

### Morning
Set off early to get to **Fionnphort**, to catch the 9:45am boat trip to **Staffa** (p127), where you can see **Fingal's Cave** (p62) and the island's famous puffins. You'll be back within 3 hours, and can then pick up the quick ferry to **Iona** (p127). Visit the **Abbey** (p62) to wander its shores and enjoy its serenity. Return in time to catch the last ferry (usually 7:15pm but check timetable in advance of travelling) from Craignure back to Oban.

Row of white-washed cottages in Easdale

# The Best of the Rest

### 1. Arran
🖫 G3 🌐 visitarran.com
Long a favourite of Glaswegians, Arran is often described as "Scotland in miniature". Goat Fell is its craggy core, while the surrounds of Brodick Castle offer more forest-path walks.

### 2. Tiree
🖫 E1 🌐 visittiree.com
Well-established on the surfers' circuit, this flat island not only has some of the finest Atlantic rollers on its beaches, but also claims the highest number of sunshine hours in the whole of Britain.

### 3. The Uists and Benbecula
🖫 C1–D1 🌐 visitouterhebrides.co.uk
A string of islands connected by causeways, with huge expanses of beaches on the west and rocky mountains on the east. This is also a wonderful trout fishing area.

### 4. Gigha
🖫 G2 🌐 gigha.org.uk
An exceptionally fertile island ("Isle of God"), which produces gourmet cheeses and tender plants and flowers, especially in the much-acclaimed Achamore Garden.

### 5. Lismore
🖫 E3 🌐 isleoflismore.com
Situated in splendid scenery, this once-important church island is now a quiet holiday retreat. Green and fertile, its name is said to mean "great garden".

### 6. Easdale
🖫 E3 🖫 Nr Oban 🌐 easdale.org
This former slate quarry has been transformed into a picturesque village. Surrounded by holes and fragmented rocks, it is a living museum.

### 7. Summer Isles
🖫 C3 🌐 visitcoigach.com
The Summer Isles are a small cluster of islands in Loch Broom. It offers solitude and stupendous views of the arena of the Coigach mountains.

### 8. Kerrera
🖫 E3 🌐 isleofkerrera.org
A popular place for yachts to berth, this green, hilly island is ideal for walking, with clear views to Mull and the finest outlook on Oban.

### 9. Eriskay
🖫 D1 🌐 visitouterhebrides.co.uk
The real-life scene of the *Whisky Galore* wreck in 1941, this is the dream island of the Hebrides. With beaches, crofts, hills – everything is just how the romantic would have it.

### 10. Luing
🖫 F3 🖫 Nr Isle of Seil 🌐 isleof luing.org
As it is not famous for anything other than its defunct slate quarry, you should have this isle to yourself. Pretty, and easy to tour by bicycle, it makes for a perfect day trip from Oban. Bicycles can be hired here.

# Places to Eat and Drink

### 1. Three Chimneys
D2 · Colbost, Dunvegan, Skye
· threechimneys.co.uk · £££
Since opening in 1985, this sublime cottage restaurant has embraced its remote location to create a romantic setting with an international reputation. Enjoy fantastic dishes, such as langoustines with a mussel ketchup.

### 2. Loch Bay Restaurant
D2 · 1 Macleods Terrace, Stein, Skye · lochbay-restaurant.co.uk · £££
Possibly the best of Skye's many fine-dining restaurants, Michael Smith's lochside spot makes the most of locally caught seafood. It may be costly, but it is worth the expense. Stay at the Stein Inn a few steps away to make the most of dinner here, as the location is remote.

### 3. Langass Lodge
C1 · Loch Eport, Isle of North Uist
· langasslodge.co.uk · ££
One of the finest dining experiences in the Hebrides. The magical menu takes in the freshest of local seafood, game and beef.

### 4. The Douglas Bistro
G3 · Isle of Arran
· thedouglashotel.co.uk · ££
This bistro offers a modern yet classic take on bistro-style dining. It serves steaks and local seafood, complemented by superb island views.

**Lovely candle-lit setting at the Scarista House**

### 5. Jura Hotel
F2 · Craighouse, Jura · jurahotel.co.uk · ££
A quaint coastal hotel, where you can meet Jura's inhabitants. Simple food is served in the scenery of the gods.

### 6. Scarista House
C1 · Sgarasta Bheag, Isle of Harris
· scaristahouse.com · ££
Simple restaurant with a compact and bijou menu. The food is sensational and the view is stunning.

### 7. Gannet Restaurant
E2 · Coll Hotel, Arinagour, Coll
· collhotel.com · ££
Waterfront restaurant serving fresh seafood. Try the local mussels in garlic and white wine or the roasted halibut.

### 8. The Mishnish
E2 · Main St, Tobermory, Mull
· themishnish.co.uk · ££
Celebrated pub on Tobermory's seafront that attracts locals and tourists alike for the live music.

### 9. Kinloch Lodge Hotel
D2–3 · Sleat, Skye · kinloch-lodge.co.uk · £££
Enjoy a five-course set dinner menu featuring Black Isle lamb or local sea trout at this delightful hotel.

### 10. Café Fish
E2 · Tobermory, Mull
· thecafefish.com · ££
Popular bistro located on the pier where much of its seafood is landed. Produce is locally sourced and the bread is homemade.

# THE FAR NORTH

Don't let the remoteness of the Far North deter you, for it is the emptiness itself that makes it so special. The dazzling beaches along the northern coastline are a surprise to many, as is the lonely lighthouse found at Cape Wrath. Further north still are the former Viking strongholds of Orkney and Shetland. Orkney contains one of the greatest concentrations of prehistoric remains in Europe, today grouped together as the Heart of Neolithic Orkney UNESCO World Heritage Centre. Shetland, on the other hand, is a much wilder frontier, festooned with millions of seabirds, and islanders who celebrate their Viking roots with a fire festival, Up Helly Aa.

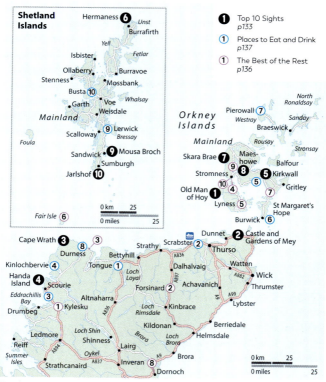

*For places to stay in this area, see p151*

**Orkney's iconic sea stack, the Old Man of Hoy**

## 1 Old Man of Hoy, Orkney
🅿 A5

This sandstone pinnacle rising 137 m (449 ft) from the sea is the most famous stack in Britain. It seems to change colour constantly as the light varies, and never fails to mesmerize. The Scrabster–Stromness ferry deviates to give passengers a view, but its best angle is from land. Hire bikes (*orkneycyclehire.co.uk*) at Stromness and cycle to Rackwick Bay (on the way visit the Dwarfie Stane, a hollow rock), then it's a 2-hour round trip on foot.

## 2 Castle and Gardens of Mey
🅿 B5 🚗 A836 Thurso–John O'Groats 🆆 castleofmey.org.uk 🔗

On the windswept Caithness coast is the UK's most northerly mainland castle, the Castle of Mey. Since 1952, the late Queen Elizabeth, the Queen Mother, lovingly restored the castle and gardens – her own personal taste is very apparent. The castle and grounds are now held in trust for the benefit of the people of Caithness.

## 3 Cape Wrath
🅿 B3 🆆 visitcapewrath.com

This is the most northwesterly point on the British mainland. Perched high on a clifftop stands a Stevenson lighthouse (1827); below, the ocean pounds the rocks in a mesmerizing display of the Atlantic's strength. At Clo Mor, 8 km (5 miles) eastwards, are the highest cliffs on mainland Britain at 281 m (900 ft). The cape is reached by ferry (*07719 678 729*) from Keoldale Pier on Kyle of Durness, and a minibus runs to the lighthouse in summer.

## 4 Handa Island
🅿 B3 🆆 scottishwildlife trust.org

Once populated by a hardy people who elected a queen and ran their own parliament, Handa was evacuated when the potato crop failed in 1847. The island is managed by the Scottish Wildlife Trust. Now it is a fantastic colony of seabirds that live here. Of particular note are the belligerent arctic and great skuas, kittiwakes, razorbills and the largest assembly of guillemots – numbering 66,000 – in Britain. A ferry (*Apr–Aug: handa-ferry.com*) from Tarbet will take you to this island.

**Great skua, Handa Island**

### 5 Kirkwall, Orkney

**A5** **W** historicenvironment.scot

The capital of Orkney is a town of twisted streets, ancient buildings and the constant comings and goings of ferries. Most striking is the enormous red and yellow St Magnus's Cathedral, built in the 12th century and still going strong. Nearby are the ruins of the bishop's and earl's palaces *(01856 871 918)*. The town museum *(orkney museums.org.uk)* is excellent, and many shops in the city sell an extensive range of Orcadian jewellery.

### 6 Hermaness National Nature Reserve, Shetland

**A2** **Unst** **W** nature.scot

When you look from here to Muckle Flugga lighthouse, you're gazing at the northernmost tip of the UK. Aside from the view, the cliff-edged reserve is a favourite breeding ground for bonxies (great skuas). Alongside these pirates (they steal food from other seabirds), there are gannets, razorbills, red-throated divers and a large gathering of tammy nories (puffins). The best time to visit is between mid-May and late July.

### 7 Skara Brae, Orkney

**A5** **Apr–Sep: 9:30am–5:30pm daily; Oct–Mar: 10am–4pm daily **W** historicenvironment.scot

Another World Heritage Site, one that predates the Egyptian pyramids. In 1850, a storm revealed some ruins in the sands, whereupon archaeologists excavated and were astonished to find a 5,000-year-old Stone Age village, which had been abandoned so suddenly that most of the rooms and furnishings were left intact. Today, you can see the stone beds and sideboards of these Neolithic people, and discover how and what they cooked. A visitor centre explains.

### 8 Maeshowe, Orkney

**A5** **Apr–Sep: 9:30am–5:30pm daily; Oct–Mar: 10am–4pm daily **W** historicenvironment.scot

This magnificent stone burial chamber, built around 2700 BCE, is a World Heritage Site. Stoop low and walk through the entrance tunnel, carefully aligned with the solstice sun, and enter the greatest concentration of Viking graffiti ever discovered. Norsemen plundered the treasure but left the walls with a wealth of runes describing the kind of boasts and grumbles that people still make today. Guided tours need to be booked in advance.

### 9 Mousa Broch, Shetland

**B2** **Apr–Sep: daily (weather permitting) **W** mousa.co.uk

Around 500 BCE Iron Age people began building defensive forts in

**The towering Mousa Broch
in Shetland**

Scotland called brochs. Masterfully designed, these double-skinned walls of dry stones were raised into circular towers, with an elegant taper at their waists. Remains of brochs are scattered across northern Scotland but Mousa is the best preserved of them all. You can only reach the Island of Mousa by boat from Sandwick, and then you must climb 13 m (43 ft) to the open parapet.

**10 Jarlshof, Shetland**
☑ B1 ☑ Apr–Sep: 9:30am–5:30pm daily; Oct–Mar: hours vary, check website ⓦ historic environment.scot ☑

This warren of underground (but roofless) chambers represents an extensive history with not one but at least five periods of settlement. The oval-shaped houses are Bronze Age; the Iron Age added the broch and wheelhouses; the Picts, ancient people who lived from the 1st to the 4th century, established their own dwellings; the Vikings erected long houses, and a farm was created in medieval times. This archaeological site, close to the soaring bird-cliffs of Sumburgh Head, is exceptional.

**Neolithic settlement
at Skara Brae**

### A DAY ON ORKNEY

### Morning

Start the morning from the flagstoned village of **Stromness** (p136) and head out on the road to **Skara Brae**. The roads turn and undulate on rolling pasture but the way is well signposted.

You'll need 2 hours to do the Neolithic remains justice, as well as fitting in a visit to **Skaill House** and stocking up on sweet treats such as fudge and ice cream.

Drive on to the great ancient stone circle known as the **Ring of Brodgar** (p136), and also visit the roadside standing stones of **Stenness**.

So far you've only covered 20 km (12 miles). Time for lunch as you make your way to the Maeshowe Visitor Centre.

### Afternoon

After lunch, take a tour inside Neolithic **Maeshowe**. It's dark inside, and a guide lights up the runes with a torch. Drive on to **Kirkwall**. Visit the cathedral and the museum, and walk the town's streets, or stop for a coffee.

In the evening, dine at **The Storehouse Restaurant** (thestorehouserestaurant withrooms.co.uk).

Orkney is also a delightful place to cycle and it's easy to hire bicycles. The car route described above makes a lovely day's cycle ride if you return to Stromness after Maeshowe.

# The Best of the Rest

**Exterior of the Italian Chapel in Orkney**

## 1. Eas A'Chual Aluinn Fall, nr Kylesku
📍 B3

Eas A'Chual Aluinn is Britain's highest waterfall. It drops 200 m (658 ft) at the end of Loch Glencoul. Boat tours *(07821 441 090)* are available to access the waterfall.

## 2. Forsinard Flows
📍 B4 🌐 rspb.org.uk

The great peatland, known as the Flow Country, offers walks among rare plants, insects and birds.

## 3. Smoo Cave, Durness
📍 B4

A remarkable natural cavern beside the sea. You can walk in a little way, but a boat tour is best *(smoocavetours.com)*. Rains cause the cave to flood and tours might have to be cancelled.

## 4. Pier Arts Centre, Stromness
📍 A5 🏛 Victoria St 🕐 Hours vary, check website 🌐 pierartscentre.com

There is a collection of British fine art here. Most works were created in the 1930s and 1940s by avant-garde artists.

## 5. Scapa Flow Visitor Centre, Hoy, Orkney
📍 A5 🌐 orkneymuseums.co.uk

An exploration of the bay of Scapa Flow, where, in 1919, the German High Seas Fleet scuttled their 74 warships after surrendering to the Royal Navy.

## 6. Fair Isle, Shetland
📍 B1 🌐 fairisle.org.uk

Famous as a haven of traditional crafts, this remote island has awesome cliff scenery and birdlife (from May to mid-August, puffins are the big draw).

## 7. Churchill Barriers and Italian Chapel, Orkney
📍 A5 🏛 Lamb Holm, nr Kirkwall 🕐 Chapel: Apr & Oct: 10am–4pm daily; May & Sep: 9am–5pm daily; Jun–Aug: 9am–6:30pm daily; Nov–Mar: 10am–1pm daily ♿

These causeways were built in World War II by Italian prisoners of war, who also built the picturesque chapel.

## 8. Dornoch
📍 C4

This attractive market town features a 13th-century cathedral, a museum of local history, plenty of shops and cafés as well as a long sandy beach.

## 9. Ring of Brodgar, Orkney
📍 A5 🏛 Nr Stromness 🌐 historicenvironment.scot

An atmospheric prehistoric site of 36 slabs raised to form a circle. There are taller (but fewer) standing stones nearby at Stenness.

## 10. Stromness, Orkney
📍 A5 🌐 stromnessorkney.com

Stromness is a charming town of flagstoned streets with a museum that draws on the Orcadian connection with the Hudson Bay Shipping Company.

**Puffin in flight, Fair Isle**

# Places to Eat and Drink

## 1. Tongue hotel
**Q** B4 **A** Tongue **W** tonguehotel.co.uk · **£**

A characterful old hotel, the low prices of which belie the quality of Highland fare served. The best of local produce is used with imagination and flair.

## 2. The Captain's Galley
**Q** B5 **A** The Harbour, Scrabster **C** Sun & Mon **W** captainsgalley.co.uk · **£££**

This stylish restaurant set in an exposed-brick former ice house, serves great freshly caught fish. Book in advance.

## 3. Eddrachilles Hotel, Scourie
**Q** B3 **A** Badcall Bay, Scourie **W** edrachilles.com · **££**

Among trees on a ragged coastline, this fine old hotel has a stone-walled dining room where locally sourced food is served. A long conservatory here is good for catching the sun.

## 4. Kinlochbervie Hotel
**Q** B3 **A** Kinlochbervie **W** kinloch berviehotel.com · **£**

With its good views and simple value-for-money food, this spot is popular for its Hill lamb, venison, salmon, local seafood and wines.

## 5. The Foveran
**Q** B5 **A** St Ola, Kirkwall **O** Hours vary, check website **W** thefoveran.com · **££**

Renowned restaurant serving dishes such as fillet of Orkney steak and North Ronaldsay mutton. It offers great views over Scapa Flow.

## 6. The Skerries Bistro
**Q** B5 **A** Nr Burwick **C** Sat **W** sherriesbistro.co.uk · **££**

Set in a glass building with views of the Pentland Firth, this restaurant serves hand-dived scallops and Orkney lobster.

## 7. Pierowall Hotel, Orkney
**Q** A5 **A** Pierowall, Westray **W** pierowallhotel.co.uk · **£**

Come here for the best fish and chips in the isles. Enjoy dishes prepared with locally sourced ingredients.

## 8. Cocoa Mountain
**Q** B3 **A** 8 Balnakeil, Durness **W** cocoamountain.co.uk · **£**

A world-class chocolatier, known for its artisan truffles and hot chocolate. There's also a range of coffees and teas. A bonus is the views of Loch Criospol.

## 9. Fjara, Shetland
**Q** B1 **A** Sea Rd, Lerwick **C** Sun **W** fjaracoffee.com · **£**

Relish the bistro menu here including freshly baked cakes and pastries, along with a wide selection of local ales.

## 10. Busta House, Shetland
**Q** A1 **A** Busta, Brae **W** bustahouse. com · **££**

This historic hotel features a revered and reasonably priced restaurant. The tastiest lamb on the island is found here, along with seafood dishes, including great scallops and halibut.

**A box of chocolate truffles at Cocoa Mountain**

# STREETSMART

*Jacobite Steam Train chugging through the Highlands*

# GETTING AROUND

Whether you're exploring Edinburgh or Glasgow by foot on a city break or are circuiting the country, here is everything you need to know to navigate the country like a pro.

## PUBLIC TRANSPORT COSTS

### EDINBURGH
**£2**

Single bus journey

### GLASGOW
**£4.30**

All-day subway ticket

### CITY LINK EXPLORER PASS
**£60**

3 days unlimited travel on Scottish Citylink

## SPEED LIMIT

**MOTORWAY**

**70** km/h (96 mph)

**NATIONAL ROADS**

**60** km/h (96 mph)

**URBAN AREAS**

**30** km/h (48 mph)

**EDINBURGH URBAN AREAS**

**20** km/h (32 mph)

## Arriving by Air

Scotland has five main international airports, with smaller regional airports located across the country. Glasgow Prestwick Airport mainly handles holiday flights to and from European destinations. Inverness Airport has a small number of flights from the city of Amsterdam in addition to flights from London and other UK airports. Dundee has flights from London City Airport. Scotland's other mainland airports include Wick, Campbeltown and Oban. The Northern and Western Isles are served by Kirkwall Airport in Orkney, Sumburgh Airport in Shetland, Stornoway Airport in Lewis, and smaller airports on Islay, Tiree, Benbecula and Barra.

## International Train Travel

Edinburgh and Glasgow are the main hubs for rail travel between Scotland and the rest of the UK. You can catch connections at London St Pancras International for **Eurostar** services from mainland Europe. **London North Eastern Railway (LNER)** then runs from London to Edinburgh, Dundee and Aberdeen. **Avanti West Coast** operates from London Euston station to Glasgow and onward to Edinburgh. Some trains continue to Inverness. The **Caledonian Sleeper** operates regular overnight services from London Euston to Glasgow, Edinburgh, Aberdeen, Inverness and Fort William.

**Avanti West Coast**
W avantiwestcoast.co.uk
**Caledonian Sleeper**
W sleeper.scot
**Eurostar**
W eurostar.com
**London North Eastern Railway (LNER)**
W lner.co.uk

## Regional Trains

Lines within Scotland are coordinated by **National Rail**, and largely run by

**ScotRail**. The main stations are in Glasgow, Edinburgh, Stirling, Perth, Dundee, Aberdeen, Inverness, Fort William and Oban.

**National Rail**
🅦 nationalrail.co.uk
**Scotrail**
🅦 scotrail.co.uk

## Long-Distance Bus Travel

Long distance coaches connect major towns and cities with each other and with rural areas. Main operators are **Megabus** and **Scottish Citylink**. **Ember** operates Scotland's first all-electric, zero-emission inter-city buses.

**Megabus**
🅦 uk.megabus.com
**Scottish Citylink**
🅦 citylink.co.uk
**Ember**
🅦 ember.to

## Boats and Ferries

There are no international car ferries that operate directly between Scotland and continental Europe, but **P&O** sails between Hull, Rotterdam and Zeebrugge, and **DFDS Seaways** sails between the cities of Newcastle and Amsterdam. Ferry services by **Stena Line** and P&O operate between Belfast and Larne to Cairnryan on the southwest coast.

For island hoppers, **Caledonian MacBrayne** offers passes valid for 8 days, 15 days or one month on its routes to the western isles including Arran, Barra, Coll, Eigg, Harris, Islay, Mull, Raasay, Skye and Tiree. **NorthLink Ferries** sails to Stromness in Orkney from Scrabster and from Aberdeen to Kirkwall in Orkney and Lerwick in Shetland. **Pentland Ferries**

offers car ferries to South Ronaldsay in Orkney from Gill's Bay. **John O'Groats Ferries** is a passenger-only service to South Ronaldsay. **Hebridean Island Cruises** tour the Western Isles.

**Caledonian MacBrayne**
🅦 calmac.co.uk
**DFDS Seaways**
🅦 dfds.com
**Hebridean Island Cruises**
🅦 hebridean.co.uk
**John O'Groats Ferries**
🅦 jogferry.co.uk
**NorthLink Ferries**
🅦 northlinkferries.co.uk
**P&O**
🅦 poferries.com
**Pentland Ferries**
🅦 pentlandferries.co.uk
**Stena Line**
🅦 stenaline.co.uk

## Public Transport

Public transport in Scotland is a combination of private sector and city-operated services.

Most cities operate only bus systems. **Transport for Edinburgh** buses complement a single tram line. In Glasgow, **Strathclyde Partnership for Transport (SPT)** runs a complete bus service, a single subway circuit and a suburban rail network.

**Traveline Scotland** provides the ticket information, timetables and safety and hygiene measures for public transport services across the country, as well as live updates on local services.

**SPT**
🅦 spt.co.uk
**Transport For Edinburgh**
🅦 transportforedinburgh.com
**Traveline Scotland**
🅦 travelinescotland.com

## GETTING TO AND FROM THE AIRPORT

| Airport | Distance to city | Public transport | Journey time | Price |
| --- | --- | --- | --- | --- |
| Edinburgh | 8 miles (13 km) | Airlink 100 Bus | 30 mins | £4.50 |
| | | Tram | 30 mins | £6.50 |
| Glasgow | 8 miles (13 km) | Airport Express 500 Bus | 15 mins | £8.50 |
| Aberdeen | 7 miles (11 km) | Jet Service 727 Coach | 30 mins | £3.70 |

### Bus

Urban bus networks are generally fast, frequent and reliable. In most cities, a single fare applies for all bus travel within city limits. Multiple trip tickets and one-day travel passes are available in most major cities. These can be purchased online and stored on your phone. Single-trip tickets can also be bought from the driver when boarding your bus, but change is not given so you must pay the exact fare in cash.

Public transport in rural areas is less extensive. Timetables are usually designed around the needs of local workers and school students, so schedules tend to be much less convenient for visitors, with departures either very early in the morning, late in the afternoon or early evening.

### Trams

Scotland's only tram line connects Edinburgh International Airport with the city centre, and onward to Leith and Newhaven, with conveniently located stops along the way.

### Subway

Glasgow's SPT subway, the only underground rail service in Scotland, comprises a 10 km (7 mile) loop connecting 15 stations around the city centre. Trains run every 4 minutes at peak times, and it takes 24 minutes to ride a full loop. Tickets can be purchased from self-service machines at any subway station. Single tickets are a fixed price and are valid on any journey. Savings can be made by buying a return (£3.40) or an all-day pass (£4.30).

### Car Rental

To rent a car in Scotland you must be at least 21 years old (some rental companies insist on a minimum age of 25) and have held a valid licence for at least one year. Major car rental agencies have outlets at airports and in major towns and cities.

### Taxi

Taxis are regulated and legally obliged to display a licence number. **City Cabs** in Edinburgh, **Rainbow City Taxis** in Aberdeen, **Glasgow Taxis**, **Inverness Taxis** and **Dundee City Cab** are all recommended taxi services.

Cabs can be picked up at taxi ranks or, in larger cities such as Edinburgh and Glasgow, hailed on the street. Fares are metred. "Private hire" cars must be booked by phone; Uber operates in major cities and even in some Highland areas.

**City Cabs (Edinburgh)**
W citycabs.co.uk
**Dundee City Cab**
W dundeecitycab.com
**Inverness Taxis**
W invernesstaxis.co.uk
**Glasgow Taxis**
W glasgowtaxis.co.uk
**Rainbow City Taxis (Aberdeen)**
W rainbowcitytaxis.com

### Driving

The journey to Edinburgh or Glasgow from London or main English ferry ports via the M1 and M6 motorways takes around 8–9 hours. If arriving by car ferry to Newcastle the A1 brings you to Edinburgh in around 2.5 hours. Driving in Scottish cities is not greatly recommended during your stay; traffic is heavy and parking scarce. However, travelling by car is the easiest way to explore beyond major cities. Roads are generally very good, with motorways or dual carriageways connecting most major towns and cities. In remote areas some roads are single carriageway, with designated passing places.

Be aware that weather can change rapidly and driving conditions can deteriorate suddenly and without warning at any time of year.

### Rules of the Road

If you are planning on driving during your stay, familiarize yourself with the rules of the road prior to getting behind the wheel of a vehicle. Drive on the left. Seat belts must be worn at all times and children must travel with the appropriate child restraint for their weight and size. Mobile telephones may not be used while driving, except with a handsfree system. Third party insurance is required by law.

Overtake on the outside or right-hand lane, and give priority to traffic approaching from the right. Gve way to emergency service vehicles. It is illegal to drive and park in bus lanes. On single-track roads that are wide enough for only one vehicle, pull into the nearest designated passing place on your left, or wait opposite a passing place on your right, to allow an oncoming vehicle to pass. You should also use passing places to allow drivers to overtake.

Scotland's legal alcohol limit for drivers is lower than the rest of the UK's, at 50 mg of alcohol per 100ml (0.05 per cent BAC). It is best to avoid drinking alcohol entirely if you plan to drive a vehicle.

In the event of a breakdown or accident, or if you require assistance on the road, contact the **AA**.

**AA**
W theaa.com

## Cycling

The trails of the Highlands are perfect for off-road riding, and there are great networks for mountain bikers and gentle trails following old canal tow-paths or former railway lines. Long-distance cycle routes and mountain bike trails are available on land owned by **Forestry and Land Scotland**.

**7Stanes** off-road trails span the entirety of southern Scotland. You can find traffic-free city and countryside bike routes on the website of the UK's National Cycle Network, **Sustrans**.

Off road, touring and city bikes, bikes for younger children, and electrically assisted e-bikes can be rented from companies like **Biketrax** in Edinburgh and **EBS Cycle Centre** in Dundee. **Nextbike** is a cycle sharing

scheme with 500 bikes available from more than 60 locations around Glasgow.

Several companies operate guided and self-guided bike tours around Scotland. **Wilderness Scotland** offers guided cycling tours in areas including the Cairngorms, the Hebrides and the Great Glen, with a support van to carry your luggage.

**7Stanes**
W forestryandland.gov.scot
**BikeTrax**
W biketrax.co.uk
**EBS Cycle Centre**
W electricbikesscotland.com
**Forestry and Land Scotland**
W forestryandland.gov.scot
**Nextbike**
W nextbike.co.uk
**Sustrans**
W sustrans.org.uk
**Wilderness Scotland**
W wildernessscotland.com

## Walking and Hiking

Scotland is a fantastic destination for walkers and hikers. Check the **Scottish Mountaineering Club**, **Scotways** and **Ramblers** for specific information along your route.

Scotland's mountains are easy to reach but bad weather can strike at any time, so planning and good preparation is essential. Ensure you have good hiking boots, warm water-proof clothing, a map and a compass. Tell someone where you're going and when you plan to return.

Walking is also an enjoyable way to explore compact city centres such as Edinburgh, Glasgow and Stirling, where the key sites are generally within walking distance of one another, and smaller cities such as Aberdeen, Dundee, Inverness, Perth and Sterling.

**Ramblers**
W ramblers.org.uk/scotland
**Scottish Mountaineering Club**
W smc.org.uk
**Scotways**
W scotways.com

# PRACTICAL INFORMATION

A little local know-how goes a long way in Scotland. On these pages you can find all the essential advice and information you will need to make the most of your trip to this country.

## AT A GLANCE

**CURRENCY**
Pound Sterling (GBP)

**AVERAGE DAILY SPEND**

SAVE £50  SPEND £125  SPLURGE £200+

BOTTLED WATER £1.00  COFFEE £2.50  Beer £4.50  DINNER FOR TWO £50

## CLIMATE

The longest days occur May–Aug, while Oct–Feb sees the shortest daylight hours.

Temperatures average 15°C (59°F) in summer, and drop below 0°C (32°F) in winter.

October and November see the most rainfall, but heavy showers occur all year round.

## ELECTRICITY SUPPLY

Power sockets are type G, fitting three-pronged plugs. Standard voltage is 230 volts.

## Passports and Visas

For entry requirements, including visas, consult your nearest British embassy or check the **Visas and Immigration** page on the UK government website. For a stay of up to three months, EU nationals and citizens of the US, Canada, Australia and New Zealand do not need a visa.

**Visas and Immigration**
W gov.uk/browse/visas-immigration

## Government Advice

It is important to consult both your and the UK government's advice before travelling. The **UK Foreign and Commonwealth Office**, the **US State Department**, and the **Australian Department of Foreign Affairs and Trade** offer the latest information and advice on security, health and local regulations.

**Australian Department of Foreign Affairs and Trade**
W smartraveller.gov.au
**UK Foreign and Commonwealth Office**
W gov.uk/foreign-travel-advice
**US Department of State**
W travel.state.gov

## Customs and Immigration

You can find information on the laws relating to goods and currency taken in or out of the UK on the website of the **UK Government**.

**UK Government**
W gov.uk

## Insurance

We recommend that you take out a comprehensive insurance policy covering theft, loss of belongings, medical care, cancellations and delays, and read the small print carefully.

## Vaccinations

No inoculations are needed to visit the United Kingdom.

## Money

Britain's currency is pound sterling (£). Scottish notes are different to those used in the rest of the UK; as a result, they are occasionally not accepted elsewhere in the UK.

Major credit, debit and prepaid currency cards are accepted. Contactless payment is almost universal, including for almost all buses, all trains and taxis. Cash machines are located at banks and on main streets in major towns, but they are harder to find in remote areas.

Tipping is not obligatory, but it is customary to leave a tip of 5–10 per cent if service is good.

## Travellers with Specific Requirements

The Visit Scotland website (p146) has information for those visiting Scotland with specific requirements. Modern sights tend to be accessible, but historic buildings may not be. Phone ahead to check.

**Capability Scotland** is Scotland's largest organization and **Tourism for All** is the UK's central source of travel information. **Disability Rights UK** lists accommodation. **Seagull Trust Cruises** runs canal boats specifically designed for the disabled on the Forth (Edinburgh) and Caledonian (Inverness) canals. Disabled parking bays are widespread but you must display a badge. The AA (see p137) produces a Disabled Travellers' Guide and also have a **AA Disability Helpline** for members.

Other useful resources for advice are the **Royal National Institute for Deaf People** and the **Royal National Institute for the Blind**.

**AA Disability Helpline**
(0800) 262050
**Capability Scotland**
W capability-scot. org.uk
**Disability Rights UK**
W disabilityrightsuk.org
**Royal National Institute for the Blind**
W rnib.org.uk

**Royal National Institute for Deaf People**
W rnid.org.uk
**Seagull Trust Cruises**
W seagulltrust.org.uk
**Tourism for All**
W tourismforall.org.uk

## Language

The official language is English, however Scotland is a multicultural country in which you will hear many languages spoken. Gaelic is now spoken by fewer than 1 per cent of Scots, and it is most commonly spoken in the Outer Hebrides. Regional accents can be challenging, even for visitors from Anglophone countries.

## Local Customs

Some remote areas of the Scottish Highlands and Islands are deeply religious. Be respectful when visiting places of worship.

## Opening Hours

Most shops are open 9am–5:30pm Monday to Saturday. City shops are usually open until 8pm Thursday and many now open Sunday, too. Museum and gallery times vary widely, so check ahead. Last admission to many attractions tends to be 30 minutes before closing.

Scotland has three main holiday periods: Hogmanay (New Year), Easter and July–August. National public holidays in Scotland differ slightly to the rest of the UK. They are 1–2 January, Good Friday (March/April), the first and last Monday in May, the first Monday in August, St Andrew's Day (Nov 30), and Christmas Day and Boxing Day on 25–26 December.

Situations can change quickly and unexpectedly. Always check before visiting attractions and hospitality venues for up-to-date opening hours and booking requirements.

## Personal Security

Scotland is generally safe, but petty crime does take place. Pickpockets work known tourist areas and busy streets such as Edinburgh's Royal Mile and Glasgow's Buchanan Street. Use your common sense and be alert to your surroundings. If you have anything stolen, report the crime as soon as possible at the nearest police station. Get a copy of the crime report in order to make a claim on your insurance later.

For emergency police, fire, ambulance services, or emergency mountain rescue, dial 999 (or 112). For medical help or non-emergency situations, dial 111.

Scots are generally accepting of all people, regardless of their race, gender or sexuality. LGBTQ+ rights are overall generally in line with the rest of the UK, which are considered among the most progressive in Europe. Same-sex marriage was legalized in Scotland in 2014 and Scotland became the first country in the world to include LGBTQ+ history and education in the school curriculum. Scotland's major cities have vibrant LGBTQ+ scenes, and since 2018 smaller towns and villages have launched their own Pride parades.

Despite all the freedoms that the LGBTQ+ community enjoy, acceptance is not a given. **LGBT Helpline Scotland** is a fantastic service that provides support and practical information for victims of homophobic abuse or LGBTQ+ hate crimes. If you do feel unsafe, the **Safe Space Alliance** pinpoints your nearest place of refuge.

**LGBT Helpline Scotland**
🆆 lgbthealth.org.uk
**Safe Space Alliance**
🆆 safespacealliance.com

## Health

Scotland, and the rest of the UK, has a world-class healthcare system. Holders of the EU's European Health Insurance Card (EHIC) can receive medical treatment free of charge. Accident and emergency treatment is free to all and immediate payment for urgent treatment is not required.

If you have an accident or medical problem that requires non-urgent medical attention you can find details of the nearest non-emergency medical service on the **NHS** website.

---

**AT A GLANCE**

### USEFUL NUMBERS

| GENERAL EMERGENCY | POLICE (NON-EMERGENCY) |
| --- | --- |
| **999** | **101** |

**NHS 24 (NON-EMERGENCY)**

**111**

---

**TIME ZONE**
GMT/BST
British Summer Time (BST) runs late March to late October.

---

**TAP WATER**
Unless otherwise stated, tap water in the UK is safe to drink.

---

### WEBSITES AND APPS

**Traffic Scotland**
App showing real-time traffic conditions and road journey times.
**Visit Scotland**
Scotland's official tourist board website (www.visitscotland.com)
**Walk Highlands**
A useful tool for planning walks and hikes (www.walkhighlands.co.uk)
**Mountain Weather Information Service**
Essential mountain weather forecasts (www.mwis.org.uk/scottish-forecast)

Alternatively, call the **NHS 24** helpline number at any hour on 111, or go to a pharmacy or chemist. You may need a prescription to obtain certain pharmaceuticals. The pharmacist can identify the closest doctor's surgery or medical centre.

**NHS**
W nhs.uk

## Smoking, Alcohol and Drugs

Smoking and vaping are banned inside all public spaces such as bus, train stations and airports, and in enclosed areas of bars, cafés and restaurants. Alcohol may not be sold to or bought for anyone under 18 and may only be purchased between the hours of 10am and 10pm, and 12:30pm and 10pm on a Sunday. The drink-drive limit is strictly enforced *(see p139)*.

Possession of all recreational drugs and psychoactive substances is a criminal offence.

## ID

Visitors to the UK are not required to carry ID on their person at all times, however passports are required as ID at airports, even when taking internal flights within the UK. Anyone who looks under 18 may be asked for photo ID to prove their age when buying alcohol in shops or bars.

## Responsible Tourism

It is the law that every person, regardless of whether they are a local or a resident, should have access to the countryside in Scotland. As long as you act responsibly, you can walk, cycle, canoe and horse ride in all open land or waters. Be sure to familiarize yourself with the **Scottish Outdoor Access Code** before you set off on your trip.
**Scottish Outdoor Access Code**
W outdooraccess-scotland.scot

## Mobile Phones and Wi-Fi

Free Wi-Fi hotspots are widely available in city centres. Do not rely on mobile phones for navigation or emergencies in rural areas as reception can be intermittent.

Visitors travelling to the UK with EU tariffs may be affected by roaming charges now that the UK has left the EU. Check with your provider before travelling. Pay-as-you-go SIM cards can be bought in most supermarkets.

## Discount Cards

If you plan to visit many of the country's heritage sights, the **Historic Environment Scotland Explorer Pass** provides access to upwards of 70 sights over a 7-day period.For travelling extensively within Scotland, Scotrail's **Spirit of Scotland pass** offers unlimited train, bus and ferry transport over an 8-or 15-day period. The **Scottish Citylink Explorer Pass** offers 3-, 5- and 8-days unlimited travel on its coach network, as well as discounts and special accommodation offers.
**Historic Environment Scotland Explorer Pass**
W historicenvironment.scot
**Scottish Citylink Explorer Pass**
W citylink.co.uk
**Spirit of Scotland**
W scotrail.co.uk

## Post

Standard post is handled by the Royal Mail. Post offices can be found in supermarkets or other stores. On weekdays, larger offices operate 9am to 5:30pm and Saturdays to 12:30pm.

## Taxes and Refunds

VAT (Value Added Tax) is charged at 20 per cent on most products a nd is usually included in the marked price. Tax-free shopping is only available for goods purchased in the UK and sent directly overseas. The retailer should remove the tax at source, though you will need to pay any sales tax and related fees in the recipient country.

# PLACES TO STAY

From grand country houses and sleek city hotels to cosy inns, buzzy hostels and back-to-basics bunkhouses, Scotland has accommodation to suit all tastes and budgets. You'll find family-run B&Bs and guesthouses all over the country, too, offering homely comforts and a hearty breakfast.

Expect to pay a premium in summer, especially in Edinburgh (where prices rocket during the festival) and hotspots like Skye and along the North Coast 500. Prices also peak over Christmas and New Year.

**PRICE CATEGORIES**

For a standard double room per night (with breakfast if included), taxes and extra charges.

£ under £100
££ £100–200
£££ over £200

## Edinburgh

### Castle Rock Hostel
**Q** M4 **A** 15 Johnston Terrace **W** castlerock edinburgh.com · £

In the heart of Edinburgh's historic Old Town, right below the castle on the cobbled, pub-filled Grassmarket, this cosy hostel has terrific facilities, including multiple common rooms and a well-equipped kitchen, alongside extras such as a movie lounge, pool tables and even musical instruments for impromptu performances. Accommodation ranges from large dorms to private doubles.

### Market Street Hotel
**Q** M4 **A** 6 Market St **W** marketstreethotel.co.uk · £££

A sought-after location just a minute's walk from Waverley station, minimalist-chic rooms with high-thread-count cottons and luxury bathrooms with rainfall showers make this on-trend hotel a winning

choice. The rooftop Nor' Loft bar and champagne lounge has fine views across the city's skyline.

### Ocean Mist
**Q** K5 **A** 14 The Shore, Leith **W** oceanmistleith.com · ££

This vintage vessel – once an Edwardian millionaire gunrunner's ocean-going yacht – has been converted into a hip, atmospheric "flotel" on Leith's trendy Shore. Michelin-starred restaurants are just steps away, and trams zoom sightseers to the city centre in just 20 minutes.

### The Raeburn
**Q** K5 **A** 112 Raeburn Place **W** theraeburn.com · £££

There's a romantic feel to this intimate hotel, once a Georgian family home, in gentrified Stockbridge. Bedrooms are decorated in warm earth tones with floral fabrics, and bathrooms feature Victorian-style rolltop tubs. The cocktails in the bar are first-rate, and there's outdoor wining and dining on the terrace in summer.

### The Balmoral
**Q** N3 **Q** 1 Princes St **W** roccofortehotels.com · £££

Built at the height of the railway age, Edinburgh's legendary *grande dame* is still the most prestigious place to stay in town. Smartly dressed doormen and concierges usher guests through grand public areas to elegant bedrooms in gentle tones and soft tartans. Relax in the serene spa, and sip finest malts in the oak-panelled whisky library.

## Southern Scotland

### Harvest Moon Holidays
**Q** F6 **A** Lochhouses Farm, Tyninghame **W** harvest moonholidays.com · ££

This is a great spot for families or small groups seeking an off-grid break. Accommodation is in beautiful stilt-mounted "treehouses" set on the edge of a forest or simple wooden beach cabins close to the endless sand dunes of Tyninghame beach.

## Townhouse Hotel

📍 G5  🏠 Market Square, Melrose  🌐 thetownhouse melrose.co.uk · ££

In the centre of genteel Melrose, this cosy, historic hotel offers good value for money in the heart of Walter Scott country. Bedrooms are decorated in mellow biscuity tones, brightened with floral highlights. Walks and cycle routes start almost on the doorstep, with bike rental outfits nearby.

## North and East of Edinburgh

### Glen Clova Hotel

📍 E5  🏠 Glenclova, nr Kirriemuir  🌐 clova.com · ££

The scenery around this fine old country hotel, situated at the foot of beautiful Glen Doll in the southern Cairngorms, is quite simply stunning. Accommodation is in cosy en-suite rooms or luxury lodges, each with its own hot tub. It's also a great choice for a meal and a pint *(p99)*.

### The Taybank

📍 E5  🏠 1 Tay Terrace, Dunkeld  🌐 thetaybank. co.uk · ££

A makeover has converted this white-washed Victorian inn overlooking the River Tay into a hip gastropub. Cosy bedrooms are decorated in soothing natural tones, with sheepskin throws on beds, excellent food favours local produce and there's a huge

riverside beer garden for summer days. It's also a noted live music venue.

## Glasgow

### Grasshoppers

📍 X4  🏠 84 Union St  🌐 grasshoppersglasgow. com · ££

Located right above Glasgow Central train station, occupying the former Caledonian Railway Company building, this good-value hotel offers sleek, stylish rooms with big windows and pod-like bathrooms. There's a cracking breakfast buffet too.

### Glasgow Youth Hostel

📍 Z3  🏠 7/8 Park Terrace  🌐 hostellingscotland.org. uk · £

With a range of clean and comfortable en-suite rooms and spacious dorms, this hostel in an elegant Victorian mansion has upmarket vibes. Added to this is a great West End location (a half-hour walk from the city centre) with views over Kelvingrove Park and a friendly team who are more than happy to offer local tips.

### Hotel du Vin

📍 Z2  🏠 1 Devonshire Gardens  🌐 hotelduvin. com · ££

Located on a beautiful, tree-lined stretch of Victorian terrace in the West End, this is the epitome of timeless, sophisticated luxury.

The individually styled rooms are awash with deluxe fabrics and carefully selected antique furniture, and the opulent bathrooms have monsoon showers. There's a spa, too.

## North and West of Glasgow

### Crinan Hotel

📍 F3  🏠 Crinan, by Lochgilphead  🌐 crinan hotel.com · ££

Perched above the northern terminus of the Crinan Canal, looking out towards the hills of Jura across the water, this charming old hotel makes the most of its dramatic location. Beautifully presented bedrooms and public areas are hung with original works by Scottish artists, and the seafood served in its bar and restaurant is fresh off the boat.

### Manor House Hotel

📍 E3  🏠 Gallanach Rd, Oban  🌐 obanmanor house.com · ££

Occupying a gorgeous Georgian house, this hotel offers it all: intimate old-world charm, a winning location above Oban's harbour – handy for ferries to Mull and beyond, which you can watch coming and going from the big bay windows – and a top-notch restaurant. Oban's harbourside eateries are within easy walking distance, and off-street parking is a bonus.

### Taychreggan Hotel

**☑** E3 **🏠** Taynuilt, Argyll
**Ⓦ** taychregganhotel.co.uk
· ££

Loch kayaking, angling and forest bike rides are among the activities on the doorstep of this stylishly updated country house hotel on the shores of tranquil Loch Awe. Well placed for touring Argyll by car, it's also within easy reach of Oban and Glencoe.

## Grampian and Moray
....................................

### Chester Hotel

**☑** D6 **🏠** 55–63 Queen's Rd, Aberdeen **Ⓦ** chester-hotel.com · ££

The immaculate rooms and suites in this eco-conscious townhouse hotel in Aberdeen's west end are decorated in smart shades of black, grey and tan and feel genuinely luxurious. Enjoy superior cocktails and good food in the elegant Gallery Bar.

### Malmaison Aberdeen

**☑** D6 **🏠** 49–53 Queen's Rd, Aberdeen **Ⓦ** malmaison.com · ££

The Malmaison brand was born in Scotland, and this playfully stylish outpost is simply the Granite City's best place to stay. Handsome, colourful rooms feature opulent velvet and soft tartans, amenities include a luxury spa and the superb grill restaurant serving some of Scotland's finest steaks.

### Douneside House

**☑** D5 **🏠** Tarland, Aboyne
**Ⓦ** dounesidehouse.co.uk
· £££

This splendid aristocratic country house hotel with its elegant white-harled façade and grey-tile turrets sits amid lush gardens in the heart of Royal Deeside. Huge guest rooms have big windows with views of the leafy grounds; there are also separate self-catering cottages.

### Seafield Arms

**☑** D5 **🏠** 17–19 Seafield St, Cullen **Ⓦ** seafieldarms cullen.co.uk · ££

Well located for touring the Moray coast, this sumptuous former coaching inn sits at the heart of pretty Cullen. The douce façade gives way to a laidback bistro bar and the cosy Findlater Lounge – ideal for warming up with a whisky by the crackling fire. Bedrooms are velvety cocoons, and bathrooms feature walk-in showers and free-standing baths.

### Grant Arms

**☑** D5 **🏠** 25 The Square, Grantown-on-Spey
**Ⓦ** grantarmshotel.com · ££

Wildlife and whisky are the big draws of this fine old hotel in Speyside's hub town. It offers a year-round programme of expert-guided birding and wildlife-watching field trips and talks and a terrific whisky bar, as befits its location close to the region's legendary distilleries.

## The Highlands
....................................

### The Ceilidh Place

**☑** C3 **🏠** 14 West Argyle St, Ullapool **Ⓦ** theceilidh place.com · £

With a friendly café, bar, bookshop and live music centre, the Ceilidh Place is Ullapool's social hub *(p123)*. Overnight guests have a choice of cosy en-suite rooms with wooden furniture in the main inn, or basic but welcoming dorm rooms in the bunkhouse opposite.

### Eddrachilles Hotel

**☑** B3 **🏠** Badcall Bay, Scourie **Ⓦ** eddrachilles.com · £££

Set in a former manse, this small country house hotel (open April–Oct only) looks over a silvery bay dotted with tiny isles. Rooms are beautifully presented, ultra-cosy cocoons. Downstairs, there's a gorgeous conservatory restaurant and a warren of lounges (one with a piano for guests to use) and well-stocked bookshelves. With off-road parking, it's an excellent stop if touring the North Coast 500.

### Inver Lodge Hotel

**☑** C3 **🏠** Iolaire Rd, Lochinver **Ⓦ** inverlodge.com · £££

Spacious, luxurious rooms with Highland-style vibes – think heather-coloured bedheads, tartan cashmere throws and dark-wood furniture – make this stylish country house hotel on the North Coast 500 an appealing option. The views over Loch Inver are superb.

## The Glen Mhor

**D4** **Ness Bank, Inverness** **glen-mhor. com · ££**

This enticing option is part of a new eco-conscious distillery and microbrewery venture. Rooms and self-catering apartments are freshly decorated with Scottish-themed fabrics and textiles and soothing colour schemes, and the taproom bar features the distillery's whiskies and ales. Free parking.

## Rocpool Reserve

**D4** **Culduthel Rd, Inverness** **rocpool.com · £££**

For Inverness's smartest stay, book into this beautifully restored Georgian mansion overlooking the River Ness. Inside, it's up-to-the-minute designer chic all the way – all straight lines and plush fabrics; some rooms even have terraces with hot tubs. Perks include complimentary pre-dinner drinks and nibbles.

## Letterellan

**E4** **Fearnan, nr Aberfeldy** **letterellan. com · £££**

With just two (adults-only) rooms overlooking Loch Tay, early booking is mandatory for what may be the most luxurious B&B experience in Scotland. Both rooms

have perks like high thread count bed linens, Bose Bluetooth speakers, walk-in monsoon showers and minibars stocked with complimentary malt whiskies. Nearby Taymouth Marina offers kayaking, canoeing and paddling on the loch.

## West Coast Islands

## Mishnish Hotel

**E2** **Tobermory, Isle of Mull** **themishnish.co.uk · £**

Tobermory's most characterful hotel is a social hub that hosts live music and ceilidhs and really comes into its own during the island's annual folk festival. Rooms, each individually styled, are cosy and well appointed, and some have harbour views.

## The Stein Inn

**D2** **Macleods Terrace, Stein, Isle of Skye** **thesteininn.co.uk · ££**

The oldest lodging on Skye is filled with character: picture log burners and candlelit tables, polished wood floors, exposed granite stonework and wood beams. The friendly bar restaurant serves locally sourced seafood, and upstairs the simple but elegant bedrooms have lovely sea loch views.

## Skyewalker Hostel

**D2** **Portnalong, Isle of Skye** **skyewalkerhostel. com · £**

This family-run hostel on Skye's west coast offers

comfortable dorm rooms, and cute little two-person huts. There's also a modern kitchen, cosy lounge and an expansive garden featuring a giant chess board and geodesic glass dome with bean bags to sink into.

## The Far North

## John O'Groats by Together Travel

**B5** **John O'Groats, Caithness** **together travel.co.uk · ££**

Book early to bag one of these colourful, Scandi-inspired self-catering lodges – they're on many a North Coast 500 traveller's bucket list. Design highlights include hammered-copper stand-alone bathtubs but really it's all about the wild setting, with orcas and dolphins spotted just offshore and spectacular views across to Orkney.

## Kirkwall Hotel

**A5** **Harbour St, Kirkwall** **kirkwallhotel. com · ££**

Watch the fishing boats in the harbour through the tall windows in your industrial-chic bedroom at this stylish hotel, housed in a fine Victorian building. Downstairs, the Highland Park Bar offers over 100 whiskies from Orkney's legendary distillery, and the Harbour View Restaurant serves up freshly caught seafood and local beef, lamb and cheeses.

# INDEX

# ACKNOWLEDGMENTS

## This edition updated by

**Contributors** Robin Gauldie, Christian Williams

**Senior Editors** Dipika Dasgupta, Alison McGill, Zoë Rutland

**Senior Designers** Laura O'Brien, Stuti Tiwari

**Project Editor** Rachel Laidler

**Project Art Editor** Tanvi Sahu

**Editors** Ed Aves, Ilina Choudhary

**Proofreader** Ben Ffrancon Dowds

**Indexer** Gina Guilinger

**Picture Research Manager** Virien Chopra

**Senior Picture Researcher** Nishwan Rasool

**Picture Researcher** Ridhima Sikka

**Assistant Picture Research Administrator** Samrajkumar S

**Publishing Assistant** Simona Velikova

**Jacket Designer** Laura O'Brien

**Jacket Picture Researcher** Laura O'Brien

**Senior Cartographic Editors** Subhashree Bharati, James Macdonald

**Cartography Manager** Suresh Kumar

**Senior DTP Designer** Tanveer Zaidi

**Hi-Res Coordinator** Jagtar Singh

**DTP Designer** Vijay Kandwal

**Production Controller** Kariss Ainsworth

**Managing Editors** Beverly Smart, Hollie Teague

**Managing Art Editor** Gemma Doyle

**Senior Managing Art Editor** Priyanka Thakur

**Art Director** Maxine Pedliham

**Publishing Director** Georgina Dee

DK would like to thank the following for their contribution to the previous editions: Rebecca Ford, Alastair Scott, Nikky Twyman, Christian Williams, Neil Wilson

The publisher would like to thank the following for their kind permission to reproduce their photographs:

**Key:** a-above; b-below/bottom; c-center; f-far; l-left; r-right; t-top

**123RF.com:** Iweta0077 16cra

**Alamy Stock Photo:** Aitan 41cla, Archivart 49br, Arterra Picture Library / Arndt Sven–Erik 43bl, Arterra Picture Library / Clement Philippe 38cb, 47tr, 135tl, Sergio Azenha 21br, Martin Birchall 37bl, John Bracegirdle 11t, Craig Brown 106br, Cavan Images / CI2 13bl, CBW 38clb, CMH.Images 13tl, Connect Images 12crb, Gary Cook 64b, Derek Croucher 11, Ian Dagnall 12br, 95tl, Ian G Dagnall 114tl, Design Pics Inc / Keith Levit / Destinations 69tr, DGB 95b, Michael Doolittle 15clb, DPA Picture Alliance 86bl, eye35.pix 74b, 106t, 119tr, Horst Friedrichs 70t, 71br, Ross Gilmore 81br, David Gowans 82–83b, Nick Hanna 67tr, Allan Hartley 38br, Hemis / Gerault Gregory 102b, Dan Highton 38bl, Historical Images Archive 9br, 10cl, Clive Horton 114b, Helen Hotson 17b, Doug Houghton 43crb, Hufton+Crow–VIEW 33br, Image Professionals GmbH / Andreas Strauss 36t, Image Professionals GmbH / Johaentges, Karl 52bl, 108–109tc, Image Professionals GmbH / Martin Skultety 73tl, imageBROKER.com GmbH & Co. KG / Olaf Krueger 90t, imageBROKER.com GmbH & Co. KG / Stefan Schurr 21cr, Brian Jannsen 25b, 119bl, John Peter Photography 64tl, 90bl, Mark A. Johnson 53t, Jon Arnold Images Ltd / Alan Copson 60–61b, Peter Jordan_F 72bl, Pauline Keightley 77bl, David Kilpatrick 66t, LatitudeStock / David Williams 111bl, Chris Lock 75tr, Oleg Lytvynov 12cra, Iain Masterton 11br, 26t, 30–31b, 104tl, Matthew Williams–Ellis Travel Photography 12cr, Gerry McCann 13cl, Nature Picture Library / Andy Trowbridge 136br, NMP Stock 56t, North Wind Picture Archives 8b, Alan Novelli 98t, Olaradzikowska 57br, Ben Oliver 68b, Oneworld Picture / Robert Plattner 35br, PA Images / Jane Barlow 76t, Painting 26br, 31tr, Photimageon 127br, Photoshot 133br, Pictorial Press Ltd 10tl, Prisma by Dukas Presseagentur GmbH / TPX 32bl, David Robertson 92bl, Seymour Rogansky 54tr, Kay Roxby 123tr, Tom Richardson Scotland 129tl, Setchfield 105br, Ian Sherratt 13cla, Kumar Sriskandan 75tl, Stephen Dorey Creative 110tr, Stephen Saks Photography 89t, Stockimo / Craig Brown 127t, Stockimo / Janderson_News 50tr, John Stuart 115tl, Rob Sutherland 48b, Timewatch Images 9tr, Nicholas Townell 99br, Sally Anderson Weather 87tl, Westend61 GmbH / Alun Richardson 55b, Westend61 GmbH / Martin R√∫ger 139, Alan Wilson 85br, Andrew Wilson 130t, World History Archive 10br, Allan Wright 113t

**Archiestown Hotel:** 117br

**Atholl Estates / Stephen Farthing:** 47bl

**AWL Images:** Robert Birkby 62t

**Cairngorms National Park:** 43cb

**City of Edinburgh Council:** Alan Laughlin 84tl

**Cocoa Mountain:** 137br

First edition 2003

Published in Great Britain by
Dorling Kindersley Limited, DK,
20 Vauxhall Bridge Road, London SW1V 2SA

The authorised representative in the EEA is
Dorling Kindersley Verlag GmbH. Arnulfstr.
124, 80636 Munich, Germany

Published in the United States by DK Publishing,
1745 Broadway, 20th Floor, New York, NY 10019, USA

Copyright © 2003, 2025 Dorling Kindersley Limited
A Penguin Random House Company

24 25 26 27 10 9 8 7 6 5 4 3 2 1

A CIP catalog record for this book
is available from the British Library.

A catalog record for this book is available
from the Library of Congress.

ISSN: 1479 344X
ISBN: 978 0 2417 0862 0

Printed and bound in China

www.dk.com

MIX
Paper | Supporting
responsible forestry
FSC™ C018179

This book was made with Forest
Stewardship Council™ certified
paper – one small step in DK's
commitment to a sustainable future.
Learn more at **www.dk.com/uk/
information/sustainability**